Small Business, Big Challenge: Providing Information to Small Business and the Entrepreneur

Proceedings of the Business Reference and Services Section (BRASS) Program
at the American Library Association Annual Conference
Monday, July 1, 1991, Atlanta, Georgia

RASD Occasional Papers, Number 15

BRASS Program Planning Committee, 1991

Theodora T. Haynes, Chair
Timothy Dixon
Catherine Friedman
Kelly Janousek
William Kinyon
Joanne Kosanke
Peter McKay

Reference and Adult Services Division
American Library Association
Chicago, 1992

RASD Occasional Papers

Published by the Reference and Adult Services Division
American Library Association
50 East Huron Street
Chicago, IL 60611

ISBN 0–8389–7635–2

The paper used in this publication meets the minimum requirements of American
National Standard for Information Sciences—Permanence of Paper for Printed
Library Materials. ANSI 239.48–1984. ∞

Table of Contents

Introduction

Theodora T. Haynes

Small businesses and entrepreneurs contribute to the American economy in many ways. According to **The State of Small Business 1990**, published by the SBA, small business has helped both employment and earnings.

In 1989 earnings of sole proprietorships and partnerships increased 6.2%, while corporate profits declined 8.3%. In the same year nonfarm employment showed its strongest gains in sectors dominated by small business, especially in services and transportation, where it increased 3.2%, while in private industries dominated by large business employment increased at only half that rate. Within manufacturing, large businesses lost 80,000 jobs, while small businesses generated 15,000.

Another positive aspect of small business employment is the characteristics of its workers. Small business is a major employer of younger, older and female workers, and even in recessionary times, small business is less apt to lay off workers.

As **The State of Small Business 1990** concludes:
"Small businesses continue to make important contributions to the economy, generating innovations, employment and income in times of both economic expansion and contraction." (p. xviii)

There is much that librarians can do to support small businesses and entrepreneurs. To help us understand the questions people in small businesses ask, and how best to help them, the BRASS Program Planning Committee has chosen four speakers and prepared a variety of handouts for you.

I'd like to thank the members of this committee for their fantastic work. They formed the kind of committee a chair dreams of, one where the chair's job is to repeatedly ask "Who will volunteer to be chosen for this task?" and someone always promptly offers and as efficiently produces the desired end result. I'd especially like to thank Catherine Friedman and Kelly Janousek for the glossary of terms they thought you'd find useful in understanding the way people in small business phrase their questions. Thanks also to Peter McKay, Bill Kinyon and Joanne Kosanke for the selected bibliography of some works in print you may want to add to your library's collection. Thanks to Tim Dixon for all the fine publicity work he did to get such a fine audience here today. And, of course, thanks to Nancy Sherwin who agreed to speak.

Now on to the program. Today, Pat Peacock will talk about the kinds of information that small businesses need and why they need it. Matt Hannigan will cover the sources that libraries can own to help answer questions from the small business community. Deborah Sommer will suggest additional places to turn for information required by small business. Nancy Sherwin will suggest ways that libraries can market their resources to the small business community.

First a little about Pat. Her expertise about satisfying the information needs of entrepreneurs comes from the combination of her career and her education. She is director of the Regional Small Business Development Center at Rutgers University in Camden, New Jersey. In this capacity she counsels many entrepreneurs, in the initial idea stage of their business, during start-up or when they run into trouble and realize they need help. She brings to this job a doctorate in education, and as a result has a real appreciation for the tremendous resources - information sources and people - available in libraries.

Matt Hannigan is a reference librarian in the Business, Science, and Technology Division of the Indianapolis-Marion County Public Library system. He serves as the original selector of computer, math, astronomy, and physics books for the library. He is a member of the American Library Association, BRASS, Indiana Library Association, and the Indiana Online Users Group. A native Hoosier, Matt obtained his MLS from Ball State University in Muncie, Indiana and his undergraduate degree in psychology from Indiana University in Bloomington, Indiana. He has served on the MARS Committee on Nonbibliographic Databases and Datafiles, and often gives talks on online and computer related issues.

Deborah Sommer is the Director of the SBDC Connection, a nationwide clearinghouse located at the University of Georgia. The clearinghouse was established in 1988 and began nationwide service in April 1989 to serve the information needs of the Small Business Development Centers. With a BS in Business Administration from Murray State University in Kentucky, and her MS is Library Science from the University of Tennessee, Deborah has been an Information Manager with INFOSouth, an information service at the University of Georgia Science Library that serves the U.S. Forest Service and the forest industry in the southeast. She has served as Bibliographic Instruction Coordinator and Reference Librarian responsible for business at the University of Georgia Libraries, and Reference Librarian and Online Services Coordinator at the University of North Carolina at Wilmington.

Nancy Sherwin has a BA from the University of Wyoming, and an MLS from Case Western Reserve University. She has worked as Assistant Head of the Business & Economics Department of the Cleveland Public Library, then Supervisor of Adult/Information Services at the Cleveland Heights-University Heights Public Library. Currently she is Public Services Librarian at the Porter Public Library in Westlake, Ohio.

A Practical Guide to Developing the Business Plan
Using the Available Resources of the Local Library

Dr. Patricia Peacock

"Today, all businesses, large and small, operate in a 'power field' in which the three basic tools of power - force, wealth, and knowledge - are constantly used ... and failure to understand how they are changing is a ticket to economic oblivion." (Tofler, **Power Shift**, p.33-4.)

As the workforce of this nation's major corporations continues to experience the effect of mergers and acquisitions or reduction in force (RIF), larger numbers of talented and not so talented, educated and not so educated individuals are exploring a career in small business ownership. But "... of the 600,000 new businesses born each year in the United States only half live as long as 18 months and only one in five lives as long as ten years." (Siropolis, **Small Business Management**, p.16)

Why the high failure rate? One reason is that it is very easy to go into business. No one is there to stop the unqualified from starting a business. Relatively few industries are regulated. And while many will continue to start a venture with no information, an increasing number of individuals may try a textbook approach to market research. And market research is probably the most important step in the preparation of a business plan.

The Librarian's Role

Frustrated with their limited success in locating data and information, the entrepreneur will seek out a librarian. Wisely, the librarian can suggest that he or she continue the process with a database search to determine whether or not the product is manufactured or the service offered, perhaps under another name, or with another application. This initial search process may suggest a manufacturer or a successful company. Use of the U.S. Securities and Exchange Commission filings will offer data on publicly held companies, while Dun & Bradstreet reports will provide detail on some privately held companies.

But this information only begins to scratch the surface. Counsel your new research protégé of the need to collect a variety of data. No single document or press clipping will provide all the information that he or she might need to make an informed decision about start-up. The point is to locate and identify any and all information. Each piece potentially contributes to an informed decision on trends and possible market entry.

General resources for tracking down information on products, services, or companies include federal and state agencies; financial institutions; chambers of commerce; local development authorities; local courts; trade associations; think tanks; trade magazines; as well as suppliers and vendors.

The more resourceful the entrepreneur, the more he or she will begin to appreciate the value of the thousands of non-traditional information sources such as public documents and industry experts. Online databases, especially those maintained by the federal government, provide quick access to information on all types of companies.

And while small business ownership has become the fastest growing career track of the 90's, lack of planning and management training continues to cause a staggering number of failures.

"Planning is a way of thinking about the future of a venture; that is, of deciding where a firm needs to go and how fast, how to get there, and what to do along the way to reduce the uncertainty and to manage risk and change." (p.239)

These are the words of Jeffry Timmons, an outspoken advocate and critic of the entrepreneurial movement. (**New Venture Creation: Entrepreneurship in the 1990's.**)

"The very act of preparing a business plan forces entrepreneurs to think through the steps they must take..." (Siropolis, p.161). Surprisingly, only about five percent of all entrepreneurs have a plan. This critical but often overlooked document has become a significant tool for the 21st century business owner. Banks, venture capitalists, and investors alike now ask the proverbial question, "Do you have a business plan?"

This paper will present and discuss the role of the librarian in assisting the entrepreneur in researching and compiling the expected content of a well developed business plan. It is not the intention of this paper to minutely define the information sources, but rather to identify and relate the variety of resources available to the plan itself. And should the entrepreneur express skepticism in pursuing this seemingly insurmountable task, remind him that while he may think he could pay a consultant to do his legwork, the finished product would probably not be nearly as reflective of his proposed venture.

The Business Plan: Definition and Purpose

A business plan describes:

"(The) ... idea and projects the marketing, operational, and financial aspects of the proposed business for the first three to five years. Its preparation permits analysis of the proposal and helps the prospective entrepreneur avoid a downhill path which leads from wild enthusiasm to disillusionment to failure." (Longenecker & Moore, p.85)

The plan enables the entrepreneur to anticipate the opportunities, costs, difficulties and requirements of starting a specific business. The best part about his planning process is that the entrepreneur is forced to build the venture first on paper. It is a vital tool! It forces the entrepreneur to think about what must be done and how to do it. It provides creditors and investors information and documentation to help them decide whether or not to finance the venture.

Research: The First Step, Not the Last

As you know, research is not an easy task. The plan will stand or fall on the thoroughness of the entrepreneur's fact finding. Every company deserves a well constructed business plan, but most often it is compiled as a requirement for financing the venture. Textbooks agree that the plan begins with researching the market. The typical research process consists of four steps:

> Defining the Need
> Fact Finding to Support the Need
> Analysis of the Facts
> Taking Action

The **SIC Manual** is the first source to check when researching a product or an industry. The **Standard Industrial Classification Manual** assigns a four-digit code which is widely used in business literature. Initially market research should include the **Small Business Source Book**; the **Encyclopedia of Business Information Sources**; and, the **Encyclopedia of Associations**. **InfoTrak** offers a significant baseline of popular and business periodicals. The industrious entrepreneur will continue his search with several of the newspaper indexes including the **National Newspaper Index** and the **Wall Street Journal Annual Index**. Libraries offer a substantial number of statistical sources including: the **Predicasts Basebook**; the **U.S. Industrial Outlook**; **Statistical Abstract of the United States** and the **Guide to the Census Data**. Under the guidance and watchful eye of a skilled librarian, trends and forecasts of an industry, as well as contemporary resources, will emerge.

The Parts of the Business Plan

To add supporting evidence to the marketing research plan, specific company information should be gathered. As discussed, companies are either publicly or privately held. There is no one perfect source of information, however, **Moody's Transportation Manual**; the **Million Dollar Directory**; the **Thomas Register**; together with local company directories, for example, the **MacRae's State Industrial Directory**; or a regional purchasing guide can provide an excellent baseline.

These reference texts and directories provide answers or leads to answers so that the entrepreneur might carefully and thoroughly address the narrative section of the business plan. This section of the plan must discuss in detail, with as much supporting evidence as possible, the opportunity, the intended market, the marketing approach, existing competition and proposed market niche, location, pricing formula, management and personnel needs.

If the purpose of the plan is to serve as a financial proposal a section entitled application and expected effect of the investment or investor participation is also required.

Through the narrative of the business plan the entrepreneur should answer the questions of what he intends to do; how he will reach his goals; and what he expects in the future. There is no one way to structure a business plan, and certainty is not an easy task.

The short-term strategic plan discusses the entrepreneur's specific objectives for the initial twelve month period, providing the timeline and budget for each. The opportunities and threats of each objective are also discussed in detail.

The financials include a current balance sheet, together with pro-forma income and cash flow statements for a three year period beginning with the implementation of the plan. The income and cash flow statements are prepared on a monthly basis for year one, and by quarter for the second and third year. Existing companies submit budget deviation analysis covering the previous year's activity. Once again, the business librarian is an invaluable resource in identifying pertinent information on industry averages and financial data. The **Dun and Bradstreet's Industry Norms and Key Business Ratios** or the **RMA Annual Statement Studies** provides financial data and ratios in broad industrial categories. Leo Troy's **Almanac of Business and Industrial Financial Ratios** offers the entrepreneur valuable information to evaluate proposed numbers against industry performance. The business plan concludes by presenting evidence or supporting documents. These additional materials lend credibility to the team and the venture. In addition, other tools of the company may also be presented, along with other significant documents such as contracts, leases, and letters of intent.

Details of the Business Plan

So, all business plans begin with a cover sheet (see Appendices, p 44). And this cover sheet includes the company's name and address, city and state, phone number, and the month and year of publication. But also at the bottom, a disclosure statement. Many of these business plans may be copyrighted and many of them, when they're used for an investor's portfolio, have statements of disclosure. The plan opens, then, with a Table of Contents, and presents for the reader the various points that are

4

covered in the business plan, beginning with a Statement of Purpose, followed by the Executive Summary, the narratives of the business, the Strategic Plan, the Financial Data, and it closes with supporting documents. This is very important, because, typically, the loan committee will only take a look at the Executive Summary along with the financials. It's the individual officer or private investor who reads the entire plan from cover to cover.

The Statement of Purpose, then, is a very brief, one paragraph statement that tells the reader exactly what to expect in this business plan. And therefore the purpose of these plans are either an in-house document as an operational guide, or as a financial proposal. In any case, the author has to set forth exactly what this business has been structured to do, the principals, the product or service. And then, in addition, if they're looking for money, the dollar that they're looking for, how, in fact, the dollars will be used, and how they expect to repay. In other words, this business plan will start out with the request, say, for $120,000 and every single page throughout, including the financials, talks about the infusion of the $120,000 and the payback of the $120,000 over whatever prescribed period of time that investor is going to accept.

We move, then, into the description of the business and your vest-pocket copy (size was reduced for distribution to the audience) of the business plan. Identify specific resources, then, that you might draw your entrepreneur back to. In the description of the business, however, the entrepreneur is required to specifically tell what the business is all about. Many people will tell you they can do absolutely anything, and, in fact, they're looked upon as rather crazy people--typical entrepreneurs--in the business world, because one can't do everything for all people, so we want them to be very specific. What is it that you're doing? And, often if they make a list of what they can't do, we come up with what they can do. How large is the universal market that they think they're appealing to? Why they believe they can serve their market. Why are they choosing their specific location? What are their management needs? Their personal needs? And the bottom line is: How are they going to be profitable?

We follow on, then, with a specific description of the products or the services that the company is providing. Again, if they've interviewed their reader, for example, the bank loan officer, they'll have a feeling for whether or not they're going to respond better to graphs and charts or better to photographs. But they should have some kind of visual presentation along with warranties or guarantees certainly spelling out the advantages and benefits of this particular product or service.

The market, then, is a specific delineation of who the customer base is, bearing in mind that the customer is the individual or the company that not only needs what you have to sell, but also has the money to buy it. So, in fact, we talk about the industry profile. After all, we wouldn't get involved with Pet Rock or Cabbage Patch Dolls today and neither should your entrepreneur. So you talk about the industry profile in the total universe, then extracting down to the customer profile and the projected universe. What are the demographics? What is the template or the cookie-cutter model that they might use to identify their customer base? What is the percent of the market that they're attempting to corner and is there potential for growth?

In addition, they are asked to also present a marketing strategy. How, in effect, are they going to tell the world that they have arrived? What advertising method will they use? How are they going to match the customer and the proposed product? How will they develop product or service loyalty? How are they going to assure market satisfaction? What PR or public relation tools are they going to bring to bear? And how are they going to do follow-up? Will they use focus groups or are they going to have questionnaires or surveys at the end of their program?

Pricing is another important factor in creating a business plan. They need to have identified the pricing formula. Will they be governed by the recommended manufacturer's retail price? Or are they going to be governed by some kind of discount formula? In addition, where will the price put them in the competitive position? At the low end of the scale? Will they be mid-range? Or are they going to be upper-priced? What are the advantages, then, that they bring to the market in terms of their pricing policy? And will they extend trade credit? Every single entrepreneur that we deal with swears up and down that they know their people so well, they'll never see a bounced check. And what is the industry model for pricing?

We move on in the business plan to discuss the competition. And in a business plan, the entrepreneur must actually identify by name and address the five nearest competitors and explain in a paragraph or two how their product or service is similar or dissimilar to what is already out there in the marketplace. Is the marketplace and the competition's market increasing? Is it steady? Is it decreasing? What have they observed? Have they any insight from observing the competition? And have they gone to the competition for guidance? Surprisingly, most competitors are more than happy to answer basic questions about the industry.

The location page of a business plan discusses the business's address. Why have they chosen that address and how will that address meet the requirements of zoning? If they need space for inventory, do they have the physical features within that location? Will renovations be necessary? If so, are the costs built into the business plan? What kinds of licenses or permits are necessary? Is there a diagram of the floor plan in the business plan? Is it convenient? Does it have safety and security for the consumer?

The management definition--the next page--is a very critical piece. It sets forth the legal structure of the company and why many companies, for example, must be incorporated because it's impossible to get insurance otherwise. So they need to have explored this. The personal history of the owner: what makes him or her have the magic and charisma to bring this venture to fruition? Their related work experience, the duties and responsibilities of management: how they, in fact, expect to structure salaries and wages and other compensations. And what other resources are going to help keep them in tune. You see, the reality is, you can't just start this business, you have a responsibility to also identify when you're going to close it. And your business plan should talk about the attributes that you're going to see, that you're going spot in order to be able to close this venture down.

We move on, then, to a definition of the personnel needs of the company and if, in fact, there are staffing needs, things are spelled out: skills; qualifications; job descriptions; an explanation of part- or full-time compensation; fringe benefits; if independent contractors are being hired, whether or not you're in compliance with the federal definition, now, of what constitutes an independent contractor; and how are you going to train your people to keep them current?

The application and expected loan or investment then spells out exactly how the dollars that are being requested from the investor or from the bank or from the parent or the Aunt Matilda will be paid back. How will you spend it? You need to provide specific lists of capital, equipment--along with model numbers and costs. Banks don't go for: "I want $50,000. What am I going to use it for? Well, I'm not sure. I'll let you know later." You have to spell it out with documentation. You provide supplier warranties, the terms of purchase. If the term has a dated capital, you need to include the dates to which the service is available. How will the loan make the venture more profitable? And I always ask folks to give us a Plan B. If their loan proposal collapses, and in today's current economy, most people won't walk into their neighborhood bank and borrow money. They have to have a Plan B and a Plan C.

A business plan, then does conclude with a summary, and executive summary, if you're looking for money. And, again, it just pulls the highlights of the description of the business, the market, the competition, the location, management, personnel, and the loan or investment.

The Strategic Plan is a very helpful tool. It forces the entrepreneur to come up with six objectives for the year. These six objectives, then, include bench marks and time lines and a budget. If they're going to spend money for advertising, they best have a budget in their strategic plan. And each objective discusses the opportunities. What good things can happen if they meet the objective along with the threats? What disaster can occur if the objective falls into play?

The third part of the business plan is the financials. And here we present a balance sheet. We also present the income statements and cash flow statements projected over a three-year period and break-even analysis. And the two directors, the Dun & Bradstreet ratios and the RMA ratios are invaluable, because your young entrepreneur will say to you, "Well how do I know what my numbers need to look like? I've never done this before." And if they have absolutely no idea of what goes on in the industry, Troy's **Almanac** will give them the average percentages for rent, for operations, for bad debt, and for things of that nature. And break-even gives them an idea of where profit is going to fall, because profit is not spare change in their pocket on a Friday afternoon.

The business plan, then, concludes with what we call the supporting documents. These include the personal resume of the founder or the entrepreneur, all job descriptions, credit reports if they're available, letters of reference, letters of intent. After all, the entrepreneur cannot sit there and toot their own horn. This document replaces them in very detail and specific terminology expressing their needs for funding.

In addition, then, the supporting documents would include copies of a buy-sell agreement, other kinds of agreements, or contracts and proposals, quotations or estimates, any other legal document that's pertinent to the venture itself, census and demographic data together with industry norms.

Conclusion

Once reserved for only the most sophisticated of companies, the business plan has become a standard document in small-business management. And while a good plan does not guarantee success, for there are still some factors beyond our control, it's a bad plan that admits for no modification, and worse yet, it's no plan that leads to failure.

Once our small-business community effectively develops its relationships with libraries, it will remain strong and viable for years. Technology does not yet offer the combination of data, database, and the professional to articulate it. Our libraries and librarians offer priceless tools, resources and experts dedicated to working in harmony to build and maintain knowledge, and therefore, our economic power base.

The Creative Use of Small Business Reference Sources

Matt Hannigan

Introduction

Thank you for that lovely introduction. I'm a little embarrassed these days to be introduced as a Hoosier because whenever I leave the state, I'm afraid that what people are thinking is this: five million people and the smartest person they could come up with is Dan Quayle. Sort of takes the pressure off the rest of us doesn't it? Anyway let's not forget such illustrious Hoosiers as John Dillinger, Charles Manson, and of course Bobby Knight.

Jobs and Wozniak did it in the garage, Henry Ford did it out in the barn and Lane Bryant did it in her basement. I'm talking not about ping pong, but that quintessentially American practice of starting a small business. Over one million brave souls follow in their footsteps each year. And a number nearly as large follow the lead of Eastern Airlines, A. H. Robbins, and Manville by closing their doors, the victims of what I like to imagine is not simply undercapitalization or poor choice of location but an insufficient number of visits to the library. If they had come to the library, here are just a few of the things they could have done:

> Analyze their customer base.
> Learn how to handle finances.
> Check out the competition.
> Prepare for government red tape.
> Write a stellar business plan.
> Identify somebody to borrow money from.
> Find out about patents, copyrights, and trademarks.

Or do what some of our entrepreneurial patrons should do:

> Check out the latest Danielle Steel novel, and forget the whole thing.

Our goal today is to help each of you better serve the needs of budding entrepreneurs who come to your library for help. I'm going to spend some time discussing the most useful sources for small business research, but more particularly I'd like to discuss creative ways to use these sources with the typical small businessperson.

As you walked in you were presented with a couple of handouts. One of these, titled **Small Business Sources** (Appendices, p. 69) is an excellent selected list of materials on the subject of start up and operation of small business. We have Peter McKay, William Kinyon and Joanne Kosanke to thank for this very useful bibliography. Think of it as a shopping list for libraries wanting to serve entrepreneurs. While I'll mention some of the sources in there, I'm not going to go through point by point. That would be a little like sending Bob Vila out on the lecture series to read the Sears catalog.

We rather glibly toss around terms like entrepreneur and small business as though we know what those terms mean. A rather tidy definition of a small business appears in the glossary you have all been graciously provided by Catherine Friedman and Kelly Janousek, to wit: "An establishment which is independently owned and operated, operated for profit, and is not dominant in its field."   This includes everything from your local florist down to a guy named Errie who sells watches from his raincoat. It does not include starting chain letters, investing in lottery tickets, or devising a new system for playing the ponies, although the odds of great financial success are not much better with most small businesses.

Entrepreneurs/Patrons

Since I came of age in the sixties as a pinko radical hippie type I tended to think of business folks as white males in three piece suits who played too much football with no helmets.   And, while a few may be suffering from an overproduction of testosterone, by and large I was pleasantly surprised to discover that business folk were no weirder than the rest of us. And rather than being largely composed of white males my totally unscientific observation is that we see lots of African Americans, women and Asian immigrants wishing to open their own business. We should be happy to have a small part in helping these folks become successful, and at the same time we probably give a big boost to the economy.

I often wonder what possesses people to open a small business. I picture them at work going "I think I don't work enough hours here, I believe I'd like to work eighty hours a week and never have any vacation", or "Gee I feel like risking my life savings today."   Whatever their motivations, prospective entrepreneurs must have energy, creativity, curiosity, courage, and a sense of humor. Two million dollars in start up funds would also be a helpful trait. They're certainly interesting patrons to work with, especially if you have the sources to meet their needs.

Types of Sources

The ideal reference book costs $9.95, is packed full of useful information and is so easy Ron Reagan could explain it to Dan Quayle. There are some books in the bibliography you have which approach this lofty ideal, and I'd like to go over a few. Near and dear to my heart are books under the category labeled bibliographies, indexes and sourcebooks. These kinds of finding guides are good for those times where you don't have the faintest idea where to look. You know the situation. It's ten minutes till quitting time and somebody comes up to the desk and says they need to do a detailed market survey and business plan on the paper airplane industry. Haul out a bunch of unintelligible bibliographies for them to look through while you wander around hoping a paper airplane expert comes into the library looking to volunteer their services. Incidentally, I make it a hard and fast rule never to use the word bibliography with patrons. Most of them confuse the term with biography as in "Have you got a bibliography of Lee Iacocca". I'm tempted at those times to say "Would that be an autobibliography sir?" Anyway, Gale's two volume **Small Business Sourcebook** is my favorite among the ones listed in our bibliography. Many kinds of businesses are listed in **Small Business Sourcebook** (from day care to service station), and all kinds of reference tools are detailed, start up books, statistics sources, associations, and so on. This is also an excellent buying tool if you want to expand your small business collection to cover specific kinds of businesses.

A particularly useful article listed in your **Small Business Sources** bibliography is titled "Small Business Matters". The article lists 35 titles Lisa Woznicki and her co-authors use in their Baltimore County small business information centers. Their selection criteria made a lot of sense to me so I thought I'd mention them. After we Hoosiers spirited away the Baltimore Colts I feel a little funny co-opting their criteria, but they are worth repeating. Small business sources should be:

Valuable for the beginning entrepreneur.
Presentation is readily understood by the layperson.
Adaptable to the needs of different types of businesses.
Frequently recommended and referred to by librarians.
Covers the many aspects of business ownership: business
        plans, financial management, marketing, etc.
Provides sources for further information or more detailed advice.
Can be lifted without causing a hernia.

In fairness to the authors I made up that last one, but the rest of them make a lot of sense.

Another great bibliography to identify sources for small business, or business of any size for that matter is from BRASS' own Diane's Strauss. (Strauss, Diane Wheeler. **Handbook of Business Information: A Guide for Librarians, Students, and Researchers**. Englewood, CO., available for $42.00 from Libraries Unlimited, Inc., 1988.) This book was a wonderful effort. When I look at it I feel much as I did as a child in show and tell when I'd bring in a ratty bird's nest, and the kid on after would have a working nuclear reactor. If you're here Diane would you please stand up? You don't mind if I give out your home phone number do you?

Business Plans

One often requested category of small business sources is for titles covering business plans. It's hard to convince some patrons that they need more of a business plan than a few lines hastily scribbled on the back of a cocktail napkin after the consumption of four or five Bahama mamas. In fact most of our patrons view writing a business plan with the same eagerness they might approach a colonic irrigation or a tax audit. However, many business advisers say that the preparation of a good business plan is the most essential part of the start up phase. Many titles are available on business plans. Your bibliography lists three excellent ones. The annotation to Mancuso's book, **How to Prepare and Present a Business Plan**, notes that Mancuso maintains that the greatest value of the plan is to the entrepreneur who prepares it. I suppose that Mancuso's implication is that after preparing a detailed business plan, many entrepreneurs think better of the whole thing and immediately seek employment at the nearest golden arched fine dining establishment.

Financial Ratios

Financial ratio books provide a set of norms so that you can evaluate the health of a given business, compared to others in the same field. The problem with most of the financial ratio books is the system of Standard Industrial Classifications, the kind of system where tattoo parlors are lumped in with dermatologists, pet shops are paired with artificial limb stores and sperm banks are listed with blood banks. Even with this limitation these books are helpful in preparing a business plan. Robert Morris Associates' **Annual Statement Studies** seems to be about the most used and now breaks information down by sales in addition to the traditional grouping by asset size. **Financial Studies of the Small Business** is also an excellent source and one which doesn't use those nasty SIC codes.

Financing

There are a myriad of books on obtaining government grants for small business. Your bibliography lists only one, titled **Free Help From Uncle Sam to Start Your Own Business**. The review of this book which appeared in the July 1989 issue of **Library Journal** was a bit more positive than Nancy Reagan's reaction to Kitty Kelley's biography of her, but not by much. Even so it is among the best of this genre of books. Some of them are marketed directly to the public on half-hour long "infomercials", television commercials on late night TV disguised to look like a talk show. Collectively they are about as useful as the Vegamatic or Popeil's pocket fisherman. Perhaps we could establish a BRASS Salad Shooter award for the biggest rip-off in business reference books and collectively award it to these grant books. At my library we caved in and bought a lot of this claptrap so we'd have an answer to the kind of patron who says "Where have you got that government grant money, man?"

Import/Export

The bibliography also has a number of excellent sources on importing and exporting. These aren't quite as popular in the heartland as I imagine them to be on the coasts. In fact in Indiana we consider it foreign trade when a farmer drives his pickup over into Kentucky to pick up some field corn. Nevertheless, we have quite a few requests for the Commerce Department's **A Basic Guide to Exporting**.

The remainder of the bibliography lists many fine sources covering such critical topics as marketing, advertising, and start up. I am certain that you will find it helpful as a selection tool.

Other Useful Tools for Small Business Patrons Include:

Industry Directories and Buyer's Guides.

The best buyer's guide is still **Thomas Register**, a source akin to a national yellow pages. Additionally, in my library we have over 850 specialized directories ranging from **Hat Life** to **Pork Producer's Planner**. These specialized guides are usually inexpensive and can be identified in **Small Business Sourcebook** or **Directories in Print**.

A recent article in **Venture** claimed that many more businesses in the coming decade will be purchased or opened as franchises than will be started up from scratch. Some of these franchises, like McDonald's, cost so much to open, that if you have that kind of money you could live comfortably in the Caribbean with no job, but entrepreneurs see things a little differently than the rest of us. Diane Strauss' book is useful for identifying these titles. Your bibliography also listed one good title on acquiring a professional practice called **Buying In: A Complete Guide to Acquiring a Business or Professional Practice**.

Non Book Sources

There are also a lot of non book sources which cover small business. Audio and videocassettes are among these kinds of sources. I have kind of mixed feelings about the people who are sold on audio and video cassettes. On the one hand my image of people who listen to tapes is based on the "wireheads" I see everywhere, people who are tuned into Walkmans wherever they go, grooving on 2 Live Crew or Milli Vanilli. On the other hand its a great way to spend time in your car productively. What's particularly amusing are the people who want to learn everything subliminally. For the few of you who haven't heard of this concept it basically involves listening to ocean sounds or forest noises, while voices too quiet to hear exhort you to get smart, rich, or healthy. I've always suspected that the voices instead of saying things like "You are a financial wizard", really say things like, "We got your $9.95 putz", or "Charmin is squeezably soft." A step above this subliminal junk are tapes by such "masters of erudition" as Zig Ziglar and Dave Del Dotto, gurus of the get rich quick crowd. With names like Ziglar and Del Dotto these are probably men who got beat up a lot on the playground and these tapes are their means of revenge. I'm waiting for a subliminal business plan tape – you go to sleep with the tape playing under your pillow, and pen and pencil resting on your nightstand. In the morning you wake up refreshed and you've got a dynamite business plan lying next to you.

Hot Businesses

You may want to buy some specific titles on the most popular businesses. While I don't have any exact titles to recommend, judging by my patrons and by perusing the small business magazines some of these "hot" prospects are:

Limousine services
Telemarketing
Mail order
Janitorial business
Import/Export
Consulting
Using your home computer
Marketing some cockamamie invention or other (Since I'm from Indiana half of the inventions seem to involve catching fish better, or keeping beer cold longer)

Dead in the water are such formerly popular businesses as:

Worm farms
Video stores
Health spas
Tanning salons

Creative Uses

A canny librarian I work with, Margaret Glesing, is fond of saying that we wouldn't have to buy so many reference books if we only knew what was in the ones we have now. While it is important to buy the latest and greatest reference book, even in a small library there are a number of creative reference techniques to use when working with patrons and sources. For example:

Next to guides and bibliographies, possibly the best resource for small business patrons is the telephone book or simply the telephone. Just pick up the phone and call up that state licensing agency, or other organization. I do this for local company information. I just call the company and ask for public relations and introduce myself. I'm often amazed how much they will tell me about the company. Maybe they're just relieved that I'm not a reporter or an IRS agent.

You can talk to plenty of knowledgeable folks at places like the Chamber of

Commerce, Secretary of State, Service Corps of Retired Executives, university business schools, and local trade and professional associations. Remember though if you're calling a state or municipal agency they like to see if you're a serious caller by transferring you three or four times and seeing if you have the patience to hang on without ripping the phone out of the wall.

Another creative technique is to use online for ready reference. It's cheaper than purchasing seldom used sources. Searching online is a cost efficient way to get tailor made information. For instance I use **Dun's Donnelley Demographics** to help people in their marketing. I know of no census source which provides **Donnelley Demographic's** combination of very up to date information, along with access by zip code and town. **PTS Prompt, ABI/Inform** and **Management Contents** are also helpful in finding articles on start up of a particular business enterprise. CD-ROMs are also great, but unless you're in a huge library which buys CD-ROMS like the Pentagon buys weapons, you'll find a lot more online.

Use periodicals as reference tools. Many magazines for example issue annual statistical and summary issues (S&MM Survey of Buying Power listing population, income, etc. is one) In fact it's a good idea to keep up on small business by reading such magazines as **Black Enterprise, Entrepreneur, Venture,** and **Success.** This is one of those things I think I should do, but somehow never find the time. Perhaps it's an activity best reserved for those oddballs among us who do handmade Christmas cards or iron their underwear.

Use other libraries in your area as reference resources. We each have different areas of expertise and different areas of experience. I often call the local extension of Indiana and Purdue universities with questions. Sometimes if I have a particularly stupid question I don't even introduce myself. I just let them assume it's a patron who wanted the material on selling diet ice cream to dogs.

Even in a small library there are tons of sources to answer small business questions. Probably 90% of the questions can be answered with ten percent of the sources out there. **World Almanac,** the **Wall Street Journal,** pamphlet and clipping files, and other readily available sources can be helpful to Donald Trump "wannabes."

Government documents - There are many free or inexpensive government documents helpful to entrepreneurs. Some are even worth the price. **Census of Retail Trade, Manufacturing, Wholesale,** etc. **County Business Patterns, Area Wage Surveys, US Industrial Outlook, Statistical Abstracts,** pamphlets from the Small Business Administration. Remember, they're from the government and they're there to help you. (Oh yes and the check is in the mail, and I will respect you in the morning).

Use non business sources to answer business questions (**Places Rated Almanac**, **Occupational Outlook Handbook**, yellow and blue pages of the phone book all can be helpful.)

All kinds of pamphlets, directories, and newsletters are available free or cheaply for the asking from local civic agencies, chambers of commerce, and trade associations. Another handout you have been given lists these non-library information sources for small business. Then too, many library consortia redistribute late model reference sources abandoned by large cash rich libraries like mine.

Sources We Don't Have, But Need

Many hundreds of business reference books are published each year. Given this abundance of publishing you might think that for every small business subject, there is a corresponding reference tool. If you believe that you might also believe that we'll see George Bush spend the peace dividend on education or that Saddam Hussein will spend his retirement doing volunteer work for Amnesty International. There are still more than a few small business books I'm waiting to see published. Here are titles for some small business reference books whose publication I eagerly await:

Something like the **Occupational Outlook Handbook** called the **Entrepreneurial Outlook Handbook**.

A compendium of business plan samples for all kinds of companies called **Business Plans on File**.

A service directory for every state, starting with the **Hoosier Service Directory**.

Robert Morris Associates **Book of Financial Ratios for Small Business from A to Z**.

The **Directory of City, County and State Agencies Dealing With Small Business**.

The **Franchise Performance Handbook: Who's Hot Who's Not**

Financial Studies of the Home Based Business

There are two other yet to be published titles which I'd be amused to see, but don't hold your breath:

Michael Milken's **Guide to Venture Capital**.

Leona Helmsley's **The Small Business Woman's Guide to Coping With the IRS.**

Information Needs

Any reference book is only as good as your knowledge of the patron who is going to use it. Some of us have been married for years and after all that time have only the vaguest notion of what our spouses are really like, so in a brief reference interview it's unlikely that we're going to look deep into the heart of the patron. Here are a few simple rules which have worked well for me however.

Never fully believe the patron. If they looked on the shelves or in a book and couldn't find what they are looking for, double check them, subtly to be sure. It's not that they are trying to lie to you, but they're embarrassed to admit they didn't learn to use the library when they were in grade school. You and I know that all this library stuff is too difficult for anyone who isn't as smart as, say we are. The public though, thinks that library skills should have been mastered shortly after sandbox and shoe tying.

Never assume the patron knows the meaning of these words; index, call number, classified, bibliographic. For many of our patrons you may as well speak in tongues.

Make a lot of small talk. People are often more revealing in casual conversation.

Come out from behind the reference desk to make the patron feel more comfortable.

Follow up by going over to where the patron is sitting and asking if they are doing o.k.

Answer the patron's need not the question (usually different). Don't use the myna bird reference technique favored by library schools, where you parrot back the patron's statements. Instead, interview like a newspaper reporter, asking who, what, when, where, how, and most importantly why. Really, they don't mind telling you.

Remember this library research stuff is hard work. It just seems easy to us because we've done it for a long time. Remember what Edward R. Murrow said about teaching people: "Tell em what you're gonna tell em, tell em, tell em what you told em."

Conclusions

In conclusion I'd like to pay homage to another infamous Hoosier, David Letterman by offering my top ten reasons why entrepreneurs should use their local library. Unfortunately I could only think of eight things, but I'm sure Dave will understand:

Eighth on the list of the top reasons to use the library; we offer lots of free pencils with no erasers.

Seventh, you can identify groups you can borrow money from without the risk of having your legs broken if you have trouble repaying.

Sixth, we've got a lot better magazines than you can find in your doctor's office or laundromat.

Fifth, audio and video cassettes: why should the inability to read keep you from your piece of the American dream.

Fourth, government documents: you paid for them, you may as well use them.

Third, find out about hot business trends such as decorative tattoos for bald men's heads, or sheet metal origami schools.

Second, reference librarians; we're a lot smarter than the idiots on cable TV, and we never ask for a major credit card.

And finally, the number one reason businesspersons should use the library, after you've lost your life savings, you can still check out a book for free at the local library.

Non-Library Information Sources

Deborah A. Sommer

I am pleased to be a speaker today at this program on providing information to small business and the entrepreneur. This topic is very dear to my heart, because it is what I do for a living. Today, small businesses should be close to everyone's heart. The majority of businesses in the United States today are considered small businesses despite which measurement you use to define them. Small businesses employ over half of the private work force. Though some researchers will dispute it, small businesses are the primary creators of new jobs in our country. Most of us, probably, worked our first job in a small business. I spent a very memorable summer helping my mother in a rural general store that sold everything from gas and pig food to old fashioned milk shakes and work boots. Jobs created and operated by small firms are more likely to be filled by younger workers, older workers, women, and those seeking part-time employment. Small businesses are probably responsible for most of our initial on-the-job training in basic skills.

As Director of the SBDC Connection which is a nationwide clearinghouse serving the Small Business Development Center program, I spend a lot of time using both library and non-library resources to obtain the information I need. In my years as a reference librarian, I never took full advantage of one of the most useful tools at our disposal – the telephone. Perhaps I was more comfortable answering questions than asking them, or maybe the hustle and bustle of a busy reference desk or a tight budget discouraged me. Regardless of the reason, I have now learned a very important lesson. The telephone is an important tool – sometimes frustrating, but crucial nonetheless. The most important things I have learned about using the telephone to gather information are: 1) it can sometimes save time; 2) people are usually pretty nice and willing to help; 3) some people are actually excited that you need information that they are responsible for collecting; and 4) it can take from five to seven calls before you actually find the person with the information you need. Despite the stereotypes of bureaucracies, I have had good experiences getting information from them, once I have found the right person. Unfortunately, the right person with the information is a different person each time you need something, therefore patience pays.

With this bit of wisdom passed on, I will now focus on the resources that are the major small business assistance organizations in this nation.

U.S. Small Business Administration

The U.S. Small Business Administration is a federal agency established in 1953 to protect and assist small businesses. With a central office in Washington, D.C., the Agency is divided into ten regional offices which then administer the District offices throughout the nation. In most regions, the District offices are responsible for the delivery of services, and are therefore the point to which you may wish to refer patrons.

It is no secret that the SBA has weathered some very difficult times in the last decade. During the Reagan administration, the mandate to top agency administrators, who are political appointees, was to dismantle the SBA and its programs. After eight years of this reign of fear, President Bush has been much kinder and gentler to the Agency and the threat of abolishment has diminished.

The following are the major functions and programs of the U.S. Small Business Administration today:

Advocacy

The SBA's Office of Advocacy was established to represent small business interests before Congress and other federal bodies. This office is charged with conducting research to document the impact small businesses have on the economy. They publish **The State of Small Business: A Report of the President Transmitted to Congress**, which is an annual publication that details the progress of small business in a given year. This publication, one of the few SBA publications that is a GPO depository item, also contains a wealth of statistical tables and information about major small business issues.

The Office of Advocacy also operates the Small Business Answer Desk which is a toll-free information hotline for information and referral. It contains a number of recorded messages that you can choose on topics ranging from loans, local assistance, special groups -- such as Vietnam Veterans or Women, and other topics. You also have the option to speak to a live person if none of the recorded messages addresses your question.

Financial Assistance

The SBA is probably best known for their loan programs for small businesses. Contrary, to popular belief, there is really no such thing as free money, and there are restrictions for eligibility for SBA loans. By law a business or individual must first seek financing from other lending sources before they may apply for an SBA loan. If they are unable to obtain financing from another institution then they may qualify for one of the SBA loan programs. If they meet certain requirements, the Direct loan program lends up to $750,000 to new or existing businesses. The applicant must be a Vietnam War Era Veteran, a disabled veteran, handicapped, or the business must be located in an economically depressed area.

The Agency's major loan program is the Guaranteed Loan program. In this program, the SBA does not loan money directly to individuals or businesses. Instead, the agency is a guarantor. It guarantees loans made by banks and other private lenders to small business clients. By acting as a guarantor, the agency reduces the risk of loss to the lender thereby making it easier for a small business client to borrow money. To apply for a guaranteed business loan, a business owner or prospective entrepreneur goes to a bank or other lending organization that participates in the SBA loan programs. The loan application process is not simple and it requires a lot of preparation and paperwork. The guaranteed loan program requires that the applicant be able to provide collateral of at least 1/3 of the amount of the loan.

In addition to the guaranteed business loans, the other major financing initiatives of the agency are: 1) guaranteed loans to development companies, which are loans made to state and local government and private development organizations to promote economic growth; 2) the bond guaranty program, which assists small contractors by guaranteeing up to 80% of a required bond; 3) physical disaster loans - such as the loans to the coastal South Carolina region after Hurricane Hugo; and 4) special loan programs such as energy loans to firms involved in manufacturing, selling, installing, servicing or developing specific energy measures; handicapped assistance loans for physically handicapped small business owners or private nonprofit organizations that employ handicapped persons and that operate in their interest; pollution control financing; international trade loans; export revolving lines of credit; seasonal lines of credit guarantees; and small general contractor loans. For information about any of these programs, you should refer individuals to their District SBA office.

Procurement Assistance

The SBA, working closely with other federal agencies, tries to assist small businesses in obtaining government contracts to provide goods and services. There are several procurement assistance programs underway.

The Prime Contract Assistance program counsels small businesses on how to obtain prime contracts and subcontracts, helps them get their names on the bidders' lists, and assists them in obtaining information such as specifications, solicitations, etc., to prepare bids. Government purchasing offices are required to set aside contracts or portions of contracts for exclusive bidding by small business.

The SBA also administers the Certificate of Competency program which helps to assure the contracting agency that the small firm is capable of performing the contract. Generally, a COC is awarded after a small business has submitted a winning bid for a contract. The SBA makes an onsite study of the firm and attests whether they are capable of performing the contract in question. Once a COC is granted, the small firm is then awarded the contract.

The SBA is continually developing an inventory of small businesses interested in obtaining federal contracts. They have developed a computerized system called the Procurement Automated Source System, PASS, for short, which lists the names of small businesses and their capabilities. Federal procurement officers and prime contractors access the system when searching for small companies to fill their procurement set asides. Small businesses interested in participating in PASS can get appropriate forms at any SBA office.

Minority Small Business Development

The Office of Minority Small Business-Capital Ownership Development is charged with helping to increase the number and success of minority-owned businesses in the United States. The SBA's definition of minority includes blacks, Hispanics, and Asians but not women.

Women's Business Ownership

Similar to the Minority office, there is a separate office to promote business development programs for women business owners. This office is also the SBA partner in the Interagency Committee on Women's Business Enterprise.

Business Development

The Office of Business Development is responsible for providing management assistance to small business clients. SBA sponsors or cosponsors courses and conferences, provides counseling, develops information booklets and conducts research into the management problems of small business. It is under the umbrella of Business Development that you will find the most visible of SBAs programs - SCORE, the SBDCs, and the SBIs. It may seem that there is overlap between these business development programs but the differences, though subtle, are unique.

Service Corps of Retired Executives (SCORE)

The Service Corps of Retired Executives, more commonly called SCORE, is an organization of over 13,000 volunteers who provide free counseling and training to small business owners. The members of SCORE are retired business executives, engineers, and entrepreneurs located in over 750 locations throughout the nation. The services provided by SCORE may differ from chapter to chapter but they tend to be matched to cases depending upon their background and expertise. To locate a SCORE chapter in your area, contact your District SBA Office.

Small Business Institutes (SBI)

The Small Business Institute (SBI) program was established in 1972. When the program was first proposed by the SBA, the goal was to use the resources of the Schools of Business, primarily students, to provide management assistance to the small business community. From the very first semester in 1972, 36 universities were involved; currently over 500 universities participate. The SBI program has been one of mutual benefit. To the business schools, it offers practical experience for students supplementing their coursework. Universities and colleges are also provided with excellent opportunities which provide community service. The small business community benefits because it provides them extended management assistance that they could not otherwise afford.

Students, under the guidance of a professor, work as teams for a minimum of one quarter or semester. The student teams meet regularly with a small business and at the end of the term a written report stating the problems, alternatives and recommendations is presented. Individual cases or small businesses are generally referred to the program by an SBDC, an SBA office, or SCORE.

Small Business Development Centers

The Small Business Development Center Program was first funded in 1977 as a pilot program of the SBA. Though the relationship between the SBDC and the SBA has been rocky throughout the years, the SBDC program has been one of their most successful programs. The SBDC program is now funded by Congress and funds are administered by the SBA. I would be negligent if I did not mention that the founding fathers of the SBDC movement are Georgia's own William C. Flewellen, Jr., then Dean of the College of Business Administration at the University of Georgia, and Reed Powell, Dean of the School of Business at California State Polytechnic University at Pomona.

The program was modeled after the successful agricultural extension service known throughout the nation as the Cooperative Extension Service. The concept was simple -- assist small business owners and potential small business owners through management counseling and training.

The program is a partnership between the SBA and a state-endorsed organization. In the beginning there were seven states with programs, now every state in the nation plus Puerto Rico and the Virgin Islands has a Small Business Development Center network. There are over 700 offices nationwide for the delivery of SBDC services.

Unlike SCORE or SBIs, the Small Business Development Centers are designed to serve as a focal point for linking the resources of Federal, State, and local governments with those of colleges, universities, and the private sector to meet the specialized and complex needs of the small business community. The major objective is to leverage resources and expand assistance to small businesses beyond what is possible with federal dollars alone, create a wider delivery system, and to contribute to the economic development of the communities in which each center is located. The services of each SBDC are tailored as closely as possible to meet the local needs of small businesses and potential small business owners. The SBDC concept has three basic components: counseling, continuing education, and research. The centers are typically located or headquartered in academic institutions, though in some states such as Illinois and California, the major state partner in the cooperative agreement is a state agency such as a Department of Commerce.

Last year the SBDCs counseled approximately 192,000 individuals or businesses and offered over 12,000 training programs. The SBDCs have always been innovators in programming. In recent years they have focused on helping entrepreneurs commercialize their inventions and organizing business incubators to provide new businesses with ready access to management assistance and other support services. Other special programs include youth entrepreneur programs, family business conferences, international trade programs, school-based businesses, technology transfer, and rural economic development.

SBDC Connection

A relatively new program in support of the SBDCs is the SBDC Connection which was first funded in October 1988 by a contract between the U.S. Small Business Administration and the University of Georgia. The Small Business Development Center Act of 1980, Title II of Public Law 96-302, (which is the legislation that established the SBDCs) contains one line which states "the SBA is authorized to maintain a clearinghouse to provide for the dissemination and exchange of information between small business development centers". From the beginning of the SBDC program each SBDC has operated somewhat autonomously, choosing its own areas of research and program focus based on the needs of their local community. Therefore, over a decade, a vast body of specialized information has been developed within SBDCs - information which was only sporadically shared. With funding for the SBDC program increasing much slower than the demand for SBDC services, there was a great need to communicate and share resources throughout the country, and to quit "reinventing the wheel." The Clearinghouse "concept" then was to create a centralized service that could facilitate sharing of information, act as a referral agency, maintain a library, and answer general inquiries. I would like to think that the Connection is to Small Business Development Centers as the LOEX Clearinghouse is to Bibliographic Instruction Librarians.

The original proposal, submitted by the University of Georgia, won the contract for the clearinghouse and stated that the main purposes are: 1) to share SBDC-developed materials, information, expertise; 2) to inform SBDCs of available materials and resources; 3) to answer inquiries on business-related topics; and 4) to share SBA materials and program information. Since national service began in April of 1989, we have offered many traditional library services. We answer reference questions, we maintain, catalog and circulate a collection, we do literature searches both manually and online, we provide document delivery, and we do extensive research when required. The SBDC Connection is the closest thing in existence today to a nationwide repository of SBDC produced materials. We have developed an inhouse database or online catalog of the materials in our collection; are in the process of publishing a book catalog of these materials; and publish a bimonthly newsletter informing the SBDCs of resources available, and of programs conducted in other SBDCs throughout the nation. We are also in the pilot stage of implementing an electronic bulletin board/electronic mail system to further facilitate communication among SBDC offices nationwide.

The functions of the SBDC Connection have evolved considerably since national service began in April of 1989, and indeed, continue to change as we approach our fourth year. During these implementation years our focus has been on providing reference assistance for client counseling and training. At the same time we have been similar to a bibliographic instruction program because a major part of these first years has been spent raising the awareness of the SBDCs to the many information sources that would benefit their programs and clients.

Our current emphasis is on gathering SBDC program information and organizing it in a way to simplify searching and retrieval to answer specific questions. At the same time, we are moving away from answering basic reference questions and arranging interlibrary lending - and moving towards referring SBDC consultants to specific sources in their local libraries, providing more specialized in-depth research assistance, teaching the SBDC consultants how to use the materials to assist their clients, and helping SBDCs establish and keep up-to-date core libraries useful for client counseling and training.

Though the SBDC Connection is currently restricted to serving only the Small Business Development Centers, we try to cooperate with the library and information community as much as we can. We can certainly refer you to the nearest SBDC if we can't help you.

Small Business Programs within Other Federal Agencies

Small Business Innovation Research program (SBIR) - SBIR is a federal program which is monitored by the SBA but involves eleven different federal agencies. The program is a three-phase award system which provides small businesses with opportunities to participate in federal research and development awards. It is a highly competitive program whereby federal agencies designate research areas and solicit proposals from small businesses. Phase I awards up to $50,000 to small businesses for research and development to evaluate the feasibility of their idea. Phase II awards up to $500,000 to carry further the research and move into the actual product or idea development stage. Phase III is to commercialize the results of the Phase II project and is generally funded with private moneys. These projects are typically of a scientific nature such as "Non-invasive Detection of Glaucoma," funded by the National Institutes of Health, but other agencies such as the Department of Education funded "Feasibility

Study on the Development of Computer-Based Course for Special Education Teachers."
To announce solicitations, the SBA publishes the **SBIR Pre-Solicitation Announcement**,
a quarterly publication that describes the current and forthcoming solicitations.

Department of Commerce - Within the Department of Commerce there is a Small
and Disadvantaged Business Utilization Office which is charged with aiding small
and/or disadvantaged or women-owned businesses in obtaining federal contracts. The
International Trade Administration and The Minority Business Development Agency,
also within the Department of Commerce, work closely with the SBA and other
agencies to serve the interests of small business in these areas. Both the Patent and
Trademark Office and the National Institute of Standards and Technology (formerly the
National Bureau of Standards) serve the needs of inventors, many of which are small
business persons.

National Aeronautics and Space Administration (NASA) - In addition to being
a large participant in the SBIR program, NASA has as one of their commercial
programs a technology transfer system. Most relevant to high technology small
businesses, they have established a network of Industrial Applications Centers which
provide information retrieval services and assistance in applying technical information.
They provide not only scientific or technical assistance but also business and marketing
information to companies of all sizes.

U.S. Department of the Treasury Internal Revenue Service offers a number of
programs specifically designed to help small business owners with taxes. Included are
publications such as **Tax Guide for Small Business** and **Information for Business Tax
Payers**. They offer tax workshops around the nation in cooperation with SBDCs and
other organizations, and in many states they operate toll-free small business tax
assistance hotlines.

In addition to the special programs mentioned, each federal agency has an Office
of Small and Disadvantaged Business which assists small businesses with procurement
opportunities in their agency.

State and Local Small Business Programs

I could probably spend a few weeks talking about the various programs
available across the nation, but each of you are primarily interested in those existing
within your own states. My best advice is to consult the reference sources listed on the
handout (Appendices, p. 80) to help identify agencies within each state that are charged
with serving the needs of the small business community. Because of the strength of
the Small Business Development Centers in some states, there may be no other major
state-funded small business activity.

I would like to mention that each state, city or county usually requires that each
business obtain a business license. A good start in tracking down which agencies

collect information about or assist small businesses is to identify the licensing agencies.

Private Sector

There are numerous associations and organizations within the private sector which provide programs and services helpful to small businesses. Several special organizations exist to help small businesses raise capital. Two organizations which provide capital from private venture capital sources are the Small Business Investment Companies (SBICs) and the Minority Enterprise Small Business Investment Companies (MESBICs). Another organization that works in conjunction with the SBA to provide capital to small businesses are the Certified Development Companies (CDCs).

Chambers of Commerce

Throughout the nation, Chambers of Commerce are one of the major private partners working with the SBA and SBDC to deliver small business programs. The U.S. Chamber of Commerce publishes a handbook **Helping Small Business Through Chambers of Commerce**. Local chambers are often one of the best sources for economic information about a particular community. In addition to their regular chamber functions, they may also provide small business training, start-up assistance, and play a significant advocacy role with local government. Chambers can also provide referrals to lending institutions which do significant lending to the small business community. Many of the SBDC centers in the nation have an office located in the local chambers of commerce.

National Federation of Independent Business (NFIB)

The National Federation of Independent Business (NFIB) is a membership organization which is probably the nation's largest which is solely dedicated to representing and serving small and independent businesses. Their services include conducting surveys on small business economic trends and studies on issues affecting small business, producing educational materials, holding conferences and meetings and publishing several newsletters and periodicals. Among these are the **Quarterly Economic Report for Small Business** which is a survey that reports outlook, credit conditions, employment, index of small business optimism, and information about regional conditions. Several of their other publications include **How Congress Voted**, **NFIB Legislative Priorities**, and **Action Report** --all newsletters that focus on small business activities and outcomes in Congress.

National Small Business United

In 1987 the National Small Business Association merged with Small Business

United to form the National Small Business United. Made up of regional organizations, such as the Smaller Business Association of New England and the Independent Business Association of Wisconsin, the NSBU offers programs of national and regional interest for the small business community. Their monthly newsletter **Small Business U.S.A.** focuses on issues - many of their member organizations also produce publications with a more regional focus.

Conclusion

There is never enough time to describe every program available, and our nation is very fortunate to have the variety of agencies and organizations working on behalf of the small business community. I firmly believe that the small business is the life blood and the future of our economy, and I am very proud to be a part of a program that I so strongly believe in. Thank you for allowing me to share with you, and I commend you for helping us to end information illiteracy among small businesses.

Marketing the Library to Small Business

Nancy Sherwin

Introduction

Having heard what small businesses need, why they need it, and what library and non-library resources are available to small businesses, we now need to think about how to get this information out to the small business community.

Librarians are doing some very innovative and interesting things around the country to market the library to the small business community.

Newsletters and Articles

Many libraries have quarterly newsletters which are mailed to every home, and academic libraries have university publications available. Put articles about your small business resources in these newsletters, highlight a new reference tool, feature resources for a specific type of small business. A number of libraries (Newport Beach Public Library, Kansas City Kansas Public Library, Brooklyn Public Library, and the Tulsa City-County Library, among others) produce their own business newsletter and send it to a mailing list obtained from the Chamber of Commerce or to a list which they have developed of small business owners. Some of these come out monthly, some bi-monthly and others are quarterly.

Business Bibliographies, lists of new business books, etc., can be mailed out to your local small business community, either as part of a business newsletter or as a separate targeted mailing.

Write feature articles about your library's small business resources for your local newspaper.

Brochures and Checklists

The Fresno County Free Library (CA) has developed a Business License Checklist and a new brochure, with a monopoly-like cover, entitled "Don't Take Unnecessary Chances with Your Small Business--GO Directly to Fresno County Library; It's a Treasure Chest of Business Information." Posters similar to the brochure cover are widely distributed throughout the county, via the Chamber of Commerce, S.B.A. and a newspaper article in the local paper.

Breakfasts and Classes

Business Breakfasts are popular in several library systems--Indianapolis-Marion County Public Library has one once a month; the Cleveland Heights-University Heights Public Library (a medium sized suburban library) holds "Business Over Breakfast" once a year and the Porter Public Library (OH), another Cleveland suburb had a Business Breakfast this spring. Held at either 7:30 or 8 a.m. before the library opens, it gives you an opportunity to explain your small business resources (& where they are shelved) to small business owners and entrepreneurs while they enjoy coffee, juice, a danish or bagels and cream cheese. The early morning hour is convenient for the business people because they can come to the library before going on to work and you can give this small business resources introduction without disturbing other patrons.

David Lane, when he was at the Kansas City Kansas Public Library, taught a class on "Do-It-Yourself Marketing" through the Continuing Education classes at the Community College, describing the resources which the library had to assist the small business owner. He worked closely with the Small Business Development Center and even team-taught one of the classes.

Fairs and Shows

One of the most elaborate marketing efforts to the small business community that I have heard about is the Business Information Fair put on each spring by the Prince George's County Memorial Library (MD). It is an event aimed at orienting business people to library resources and services. It is held for two days, 9 a.m. to 9 p.m., specifically targeting small business planners and owners. They have a key note speaker and ten mini seminars including "Financing a Small Business in Maryland", "Doing Business with Prince George's County" and "Market Research Using Library Resources" They have "Information Stations" with hundreds of resources on business planning, marketing and sales, home-based business, business writing, ideas for small business, etc., etc. Books were displayed at each "Information Station", with multiple copies in piles as well as displayed face out like a bookstore. Mini bibliographies, in bookmark format, were produced for each topic.

On a smaller scale, libraries can ask to have a booth at local Business to Business Shows. The Cleveland Public Library has had a display in a Business to Business Show in downtown Cleveland and the Cleveland Heights-University Heights Public Library has participated in suburban Business to Business Shows. People are often surprised to see the library at such shows, but you can really impress them with a sampling of business reference material and book lists. Some libraries have even developed a video which they show in trade show booths.

Workshops

In Cleveland, C.O.S.E. (the Council of Smaller Enterprises), the small business section of the Chamber of Commerce, puts on numerous small business workshops and seminars for which another librarian and I have produced bibliographies. Each fall C.O.S.E. puts on an extensive two day Entrepreneurship Conference for which I have produced the bibliography for the notebook which each participant receives. Another librarian and I gathered books and materials for a "Resource Center" at the Conference. When the participants came into the room we were able to tell them about small business materials which they could find at their local library.

Government Resources

You could tell from what Deb Sommer has told you that the Small Business Development Centers are excellent small business resources. If there is a SBDC near you, needless to say, you should work closely with the SBDC staff.

The Toledo/Lucas County Public Library has a very successful Government Procurement Center which helps small businesses gain government contracts. The library's statistics show what a positive impact their Government Procurement Center has had on the local economy, too. Of course these facts have been publicized in the local paper.

Service to Area Industries

Look for industries in your area which you can serve. The Central Library of Portland's Multnomah County Library serves the construction industry. This service has become a two-way street, as construction associations have contributed material to the Central Library of Portland.

Directories and Bookmarks

Baltimore County Public Library publishes a "Resource Directory for the Small Business Owner in Baltimore County" (in its third edition) in cooperation with the Baltimore County Chamber of Commerce, Small Business Council and the Baltimore County Economic Development Commission. This 69 page Directory has been funded by the First National Bank of Maryland. This directory refers business owners to local agencies and organizations which provide counseling and information to assist in the management and planning of a business, giving local contacts/resources as well as listing books which are in the library. The Directory is divided into subject categories, with one Appendix listing local and national professional organizations and another Appendix giving a step-by-step guide to starting a business in Baltimore County. The Baltimore County Public Library also received an LSCA grant in 1986 which enabled them to designate three branches as Small Business Matters Centers. In addition to offering public information programs for the entrepreneur, these branches have created a special display/work area for their small business patrons.

Have banks include a small library flyer or book mark in their bank statement mailings.

Speakers and Committees

Business librarians are speakers at SCORE workshops and/or they have arranged to have SCORE present their workshops in the library. Always be a part of these workshops, describing the library's small business resources.

The library could also sponsor small business related seminars or workshops, with well known and well qualified speakers – a lawyer, an accountant, a banker, a tax specialist, etc.

Speak at Rotary, Kiwanis, Chamber of Commerce, business and professional groups, etc. These groups are always looking for programs and this gives you a wonderful opportunity to "sell" the library and its small business resources.

Prince George's County Memorial Library (MD) has formed a "Business Industry Group in Support of Libraries". When they began to recruit people for the Library's business advisory group, they focused on young business people, the type that were not on every committee. They found a group who wanted to become involved and who will probably continue their ties with the Library for many years. Once this group was formed, the first thing the library staff did was to present an orientation to the group on library services. They realized that these business people, just like the general public, were not aware of the many available library services. Prince George's County Memorial Library is using this business group to help promote and market the library to the community. The business community had recognized their need to be involved with the schools; so the library was a natural tie-in with education.

Conclusion

Yes, there are many ways that we can market the library to the small business community. Use one or more of these ideas or be creative and come up with a new idea. It is important for us to get out and "sell" the library. We all know that the library is one of the best kept secrets, especially in the small business community.

QUESTIONS, ANSWERS AND SUGGESTIONS

THEO: Thank you very much, Nancy, for all those good suggestions. We will now entertain any questions that you have. Someone up here will repeat the questions, since we understand it's often difficult for everyone in the room to hear speakers from the floor. Also, we hope that if you've enjoyed today's program, you will want to become involved in BRASS, and the fastest way to do that is to stick around for the membership meeting that will be held here starting about 12:00 noon. Anybody have any questions? Yes, in the green shirt?

Q: The question is: Can you reproduce the handout?
A: (Theo) Yes, go right ahead.

S: (Theo) Could people hear that suggestion in the back? Okay. He's saying that one way to cut through being referred over and over again, if you call an agency or a company for information directly, is to start by contacting the librarian within that organization. And that the way to get the names for the librarians is Gale's **Directory of Special Libraries** and professional association membership directories is the other way to get to those people. And local lists.

Q & A: (Pat) If I could address some of that, what I would recommend, if you have an individual with difficulty in English, as a primary language, refer them to a Small Business Development Center. We have access to translators. It would be no problem, in addition to which, even if you gave them a translated book, they probably couldn't tie in the references or the relationships or whatever. So we have materials, in addition to which Deborah can get some for you from the SBDC Connection, translations of many of the SBDC publications in the Indo-Chinese and Vietnamese languages. They've already been done; we did a special project about three years ago in New Jersey with that. So if she doesn't have them, we have them in New Jersey, okay?

Additional: (Deb) Pat answered the question mostly. We also have a number of materials in Spanish. The Puerto Rican and some of the Western Texas SBDCs have translated either Small Business Administration **Management Aids**, or they've developed entire workbooks. So we probably are a unique resource for that type of material. Or, we can refer you to the SBDC who does produce that, and they'll probably sell it to you.

Q & A: (Deb) Some of the Small Business Development Centers throughout the country have developed things like that, and we are the repository for that group. I'll go ahead and give you our 800 number. It's 800 ... I never call it, so I don't know it ... 800-633-6450, and probably your best bet would be to ask for me or for Tim Dixon over there who is one of the librarians, because our secretary screens calls.

Q: (Pat) The question is: When you get people who come into the library who particularly request the **Catalog of Federal Domestic Assistance** or other hard-to-use materials, is that the appropriate way to go, to turn this information over to them? Or does one first refer them to SBA or SCORE or an organization like that?

A: (Pat) On behalf of the SBDCs, I would say absolutely every librarian -- I think you people are priceless -- every librarian should feel very comfortable making a contact with your SBDC the first thing next Monday morning, after the Fourth of July holiday, and introduce yourselves. Because we need you as badly as you need to know that you can refer people to us. And people who are starting a small business, invariably are looking for quick ways to get started. They want the fastest way to a dollar bill. And that's why they're going to these catalogs of assistance. There is no short-cut way around it. So if you refer them for the counseling program, our counseling services are absolutely, 100% free, and in all fifty states and the possessions that have SBDCs. There are small charges for training, but the counseling is all free. No question is a stupid question. SBDCs typically schedule on an appointment basis only. So if that's the nature of your question; if they're looking to do exporting business, or if they want to get rich on importing, send them to an SBDC so that we can help them understand all of the dynamics that go into, first of all, getting yourself legitimate in order to be able to call yourself a company, and then getting involved with anything that has to do with government regulation or red tape, and importing and exporting are fraught with that, as an example. Or if they want to do day-care, or absolutely anything else. But put them in touch with us.

Q: Deb, would you add anything else?

A: (Deb) Yeah, I'd add one thing. The librarians of the SBDC Connection hate to use the **Catalog of Federal Domestic Assistance**, and so we avoid it as much as possible. And, Tim, I'm not sure I remember the source that we used. It's in a notebook, your typical librarian notebook. Yeah, it's put out by Government Information Services; I think it's called their **Federal Funding Guide**. And it's in a much more usable format. I mean, you can read it without a magnifying glass, and it has a pretty good index. And they also publish a couple of other sort of complementary services like the **Minority Funding Report**, and I don't know how many others. And we find those real useful. And a lot of times, if you contact your SBDC ... I think Pat is an exception. She uses library resources a lot, probably has access to good libraries. But some of you who are in very rural areas may not, your SBDCs may not have access to those. If they've not heard of the SBDC Connection--and some of them haven't--give them our 800 number, and tell them to call us if they need the information.

Q & A: (Theo) Unfortunately, you're going to have to pay. Fortunately, there are bunches of them on chairs over here. Does anybody else have any questions or comments? Yes.

S: A person in the audience addresses a situation about the **Catalog of Federal Domestic Assistance** and tells that he can show how to use this catalog in about two minutes. It's not that difficult to use. It also includes the telephone number of the person who runs the grant. The person will tell you how to fill out the grant to get the money. So, there are lots of ways to use government publications. Since you did pay for them, you might as well use them without having to go through an 800 number and wait for somebody in Washington who may or may not be able to help you.

Q & A: (Nancy) Are you from there? I was actually ... I could see my timekeeper waiving in front of me, and my eye slipped down. What I was going to mention with them was the interesting thing I heard about working with a specific industry, and how out there, they have, for obvious reasons, concentrated on the construction and lumber industry. And they have, at one of the lumber associations, managed to work a two-way street. The industry gives the Multnomah County Public Library a gift to enable them to purchase more books on that particular subject area. So, the point I was going to make, was to pick out if there is a particular industry in your area, concentrate on reaching out to them, work with them. And you may find that they, as a company, or if there's an association if there's a large enough industry gathering in that area, the association may show their thanks to you by making gifts to your library.

Q & A: (Matt) The question is that I had mentioned using on-line rather than CD-ROMS. As far as searching on-line rather than purchasing seldom-used sources, I think that is very nearly always cost-efficient. We spend about $12,000 a year doing on-line ready reference. And we're very liberal in our definition of on-line, ready reference. Basically, if they can't find the material in the CD-ROMS or the books, we try to volunteer to search for the material on-line. In terms of the second part of your question may imply: How does one make a choice between online or CD-ROM for a particular product? I think you should only buy a CD-ROM product if it's going to be in constant use. And however that's figured out is difficult. Sometimes you have to buy it and be willing to trash it after a year. And that's difficult for libraries to do sometimes.

THEO: Okay. Well, if that's all of the questions from the floor, I'd like to turn the podium over to Craig Hawbaker, who is now going to conduct the membership meeting.

SMALL BUSINESS, BIG CHALLENGE: THE VOCABULARY OF SMALL BUSINESS AND THE ENTREPRENEUR

A glossary to help librarians better understand the terminology used by entrepreneurs and others seeking small business information

Catherine Friedman and Kelly Janousek

SMALL BUSINESS -- An establishment which is independently owned and operated, operated for profit, and is not dominant in its field.

ENTREPRENEUR -- Small business owner. The one who owns, organizes, manages, and assumes the risks of a small business.

ACE   See Active Corps of Executives

ACTIVE CORPS OF EXECUTIVES (also known as ACE) -- Organization of volunteers who provide counseling and teach seminars for small firms. See also Service Corps of Retired Executives.

ASSETS -- Anything of value owned by a company.

BALANCE SHEET -- A financial statement that lists the total assets and total liabilities of a company at a given time.

BRAND NAME -- The part of a brand, trademark or service mark that can be spoken. It can be a word, letter, or group of words or letters.

BRIDGE FINANCING (also known as a Swing Loan) -- A short term loan made in expectation of intermediate-term or long-term financing. Can be used when a company plans to go public in near future.

Business Incubator   See Incubator

BUSINESS LICENSE (also known as a Business Permit) -- Permission granted by an authorized official (city, state, or federal government) to a company allowing it to engage in a specified business activity. A license for certain business activities is required by law.

BUSINESS NAME -- A registered business name usually found on a "doing business as..." (D.B.A.) form filed with local government. It prevents any other business from using that same name for a similar business in the same locale.

Business Norms   See Financial Ratios

BUSINESS PLAN (also called a Business Proposal) -- A document that spells out a company's expected course of action for a specified period, usually including a detailed listing and analysis of risks and uncertainties. For the small business, it ideally should examine the proposed products, the market, the industry, the management policies, the marketing policies, production needs, and financial needs. Frequently it is used as a prospectus for potential investors and lenders.

CAPITAL -- The money needed to run a business, usually gathered via various loan opportunities.

CLOSELY HELD CORPORATION (also known as a Close Corporation) -- A corporation, the shares of which are held by a few persons, usually officers, employees, or others close to the management, and are rarely offered to the public. In almost all cases, financial information for these companies is difficult to find.

COMPANY -- A group of people organized together to carry on some business activity. See also Corporation.

CORPORATION -- A legal entity chartered by state or federal government, and legally separate from the persons who own it. Corporation owners, officers and directors are not usually liable for the corporation's debt.

COTTAGE INDUSTRY -- Business based in the home in which the family unit is the labor force and family-owned equipment is used to process the goods. See also Home-Based Business.

CREDIT RATING -- A letter or number calculated by an organization (for example, Dun & Bradstreet) to represent the ability and disposition of a business to meet its financial obligations.

Doing Business As (also known as D.B.A.) See Business Name

ENTERPRISE (also called Branches, Places of Business) -- A business organization consisting of one or more establishments under the same ownership or control. See also Establishment.

EQUITY FINANCING -- Raising money by selling part of the ownership of a company.

EQUITY PARTNERSHIP -- A limited partnership arrangement for providing start-up and seed capital to businesses.

ESTABLISHMENT (also called Single-Establishment Enterprise) -- Firms or businesses of any one single physical location where business is conducted. Data in **County Business Patterns** by U.S. Bureau of Census is counted by number of establishments. See also Enterprise.

FEASIBILITY STUDY -- A study to determine the likelihood that a proposed product or development will fulfill the objectives of a particular investor.

FINANCIAL ANALYSIS -- The techniques used to determine money needs in a business. These techniques include ratio analysis, calculation of return-on-investment, guides for measuring profitability, and break even analysis to determine ultimate success.

FINANCIAL RATIOS, CORPORATE (also called Financial Averages, Operating Ratios, Business Ratios) -- A relationship between key financial figures found in a company's financial statement. The relationship is in the form of a numeric value and is used to evaluate risk and how a company is performing.

FINANCIAL RATIOS, INDUSTRY (also called Industrial Averages, Industry Ratios, Financial Averages, Business or Industrial Norms) -- Corporate financial ratios averaged for a specified industry. These are used for comparison purposes and reveal industry trends and identify differences between the performance of a specific company and the performance of its industry.

FIRST-STAGE FINANCING (also know as First-Round Financing) -- Financing provided to companies that have expended their initial capital (often in developing and market testing a prototype), and require funds to initiate full-scale manufacturing and sales.

FRANCHISING -- A form of license granted by a company (the franchiser) to an individual or firm (the franchisee) to operate a business, or distribute or market a product, method or service. The franchisee agrees to use the franchiser's name, products, promotions, services, and marketing strategies. A franchise can also be a right for an affiliated dealer (franchisee) to market a franchiser's goods or services in an defined geographic area.

GOING PUBLIC -- Phrase used when a company decides to sell stock to the public for the first time therefore becoming a publicly held corporation.

HOME-BASED BUSINESS -- Gainful employment carried on in the home. See also Cottage Industry.

INCOME -- Money or its equivalent, earned or accrued, resulting from the sale of goods and services.

INCOME STATEMENT -- Financial statement that lists the profits and losses of a company at a given time.

INCORPORATION -- Process by which a company receives its authorization by a state to operate as a corporation.

INCUBATOR -- A privately-funded, nonprofit corporation designed to assist entrepreneurs in developing business skills in an environment that promotes company development. Incubators can provide secretarial support, administrative assistance, facilities support, and business expertise.

Industrial Averages, Industry Ratios, Industrial Norms See Financial Ratios

IPO/INITIAL PUBLIC OFFERING -- Corporation's first offering of stock to the public.

JOINT VENTURE -- This occurs when two or more people combine efforts in a particular business enterprise, usually a single transaction or a limited activity, and agree to share the profits and losses jointly or in proportion to their contributions.

LIABILITIES -- Amount of money owed by a company either as debt or obligations.

LIMITED PARTNERSHIP -- For liability, a hybrid between a partnership and a corporation. Limited partners contribute capital, share in profits and losses but by law can not participate in management in any way and incur no liability with respect to partnership obligations beyond contribution of capital.

MARKET RESEARCH -- A systematic collection, analysis and reporting of data about the market and its preferences, opinions, trends and plans. Used for corporate decision-making.

MOM & POP BUSINESS -- A small store or enterprise having limited capital, principally employing family members.

NET ASSETS (also known as Net Worth) -- Difference between a company's total assets and its total liabilities.

NET INCOME (also known as Net Earnings) -- The amount remaining from earnings and profits after all expenses and costs have been met or deducted.

Operating Ratios   See Financial Ratios

PARTNERSHIP -- This is defined as "an association of two or more persons to carry on as co-owners of a business for profits." Each partner is responsible for the debts of the partnership.

PATENT -- A granting of a property right by the Government to the inventor "to exclude others from making , using, or selling the invention." Lasts for 17 years, 14 years for design patents. After expiration of the term the patentee loses right to the invention.

PROFESSIONAL CORPORATION -- Organized by members of a profession such as medicine, dentistry, or law for the purpose of conducting their professional activities as a corporation. Liability of a member or shareholder is limited in the same manner as in a business corporation.

PROFIT AND LOSS STATEMENT (also known as P & L or Income and Expense Statement) -- Summary of the incomes (total revenues) and costs of a company's operation during a specific period of time.

Private Company   See Closely Held Corporation

PRIVATE PLACEMENT (also known as Private Financing or Private Offering) -- A way of raising capital by offering for sale an investment or business to a small group of investors generally avoiding registration with the Securities and Exchange Commission or state securities registration agencies.

PUBLICLY HELD CORPORATION (also called Public Company) -- A corporation that has permission from the federal government to sell securities, stocks in particular, to the general public. It must meet certain disclosure requirements and is regulated by the Securities and Exchange Commission.

RESEARCH AND DEVELOPMENT FINANCING -- Tax advantaged partnership set up to finance product development for start-ups as well as more mature companies.

RISK CAPITAL -- Funds invested with the hope of some yield or income from an enterprise in which the investor has no control.

"S" CORPORATION (formally called "Sub Chapter S" corporation) -- In general, a corporation that has elected to have its income taxed to the shareholders as if the corporation were a partnership. This avoids the double taxation inherent in the taxation of corporations. A small business must fulfill several requirements before it can operate as an "S" corporation.

SALES -- Income received by a company in exchange for goods and services.

SBA   See Small Business Administration

SBDC   See Small Business Development Centers

SBI   See Small Business Institutes

SBIC   See Small Business Investment Companies

SCORE   See Service Corp of Retired Executives

SECOND-STAGE FINANCING (also known as Second-Round Financing) -- Working capital for the initial expansion of a company that is producing and shipping and has growing accounts receivable and inventories. Although company has made progress, it may not yet be showing a profit.

SEED FINANCING -- Relatively small amount of money used at the preliminary organizing and planning stages of a business.

SERVICE CORPS OF RETIRED EXECUTIVES (also known as SCORE) -- Organization that provides volunteers in management assistance programs of the SBA. See also Active Corps of Executives.

SIC   See Standard Industrial Classification System

SMALL BUSINESS ADMINISTRATION (also known as SBA) -- Independent agency of the federal government which provides assistance in loans, management, and advocating interests before other federal agencies. See also Small Business Investment Companies.

SMALL BUSINESS DEVELOPMENT CENTERS (also known as SBDCs) -- Centers that provide support services to small businesses including individual counseling, SBA advice, seminars, conferences, and learning center activities. Most services are free of charge or available at minimal cost.

SMALL BUSINESS INSTITUTES (also called SBIs) -- Cooperative arrangements made between SBA district offices and local colleges and universities to provide small business firms with support services, including graduate students who provide inexpensive counseling, facilities, administrative support, and special contacts. See also Incubator.

SMALL BUSINESS INVESTMENT COMPANIES (also called SBICs) -- These SBA regulated and sponsored firms provide money or venture capital to small businesses under a variety of agreements. See also Small Business Development Centers and Venture Capital.

SOLE PROPRIETORSHIP -- Simplest legal structure of a business, generally requiring only a local business license to operate. From a tax standpoint, the individual owner and the business are the same.

STANDARD INDUSTRIAL CLASSIFICATION SYSTEM (also called SIC Code) -- A numbering system established by the federal government and used to categorize businesses by type of economic activity.

START-UP FINANCING -- Financing provided to companies either completing product development and initial marketing or already in business for one year or less, but have not sold their product commercially.

TARGET MARKET -- The clients or customers sought for a business' product or service.

THIRD-STAGE FINANCING (also known as Third-Round or Mezzanine Financing) -- Financing provided for major expansion of a company whose sales volume is increasing and that is breaking even or profitable. These funds are used for further plant expansion, marketing, working capital, or development of an improved product.

TRADE NAME -- The name under which a company conducts business, or by which its business, goods or services are identified. It may or may not be registered as a trademark.

TRADEMARK -- Federal statues allow a trademark to be registered by its owner or user. It can be a word, symbol, design or combination word and design, slogan or even a distinctive sound which identifies and distinguishes the goods and services of one party from those of another. The term of a trademark is 10 years with 10 year renewals.

VENTURE CAPITAL -- Source of financing for start-up companies and others embarking on new, turnaround, or expanding ventures that entail some investment risk, but offer above-average future profits.

WORKING CAPITAL -- Name refers to a firm's short-term investment of current assets, including cash, short-term securities, accounts receivable and inventories.

BIBLIOGRAPHY OF SOURCES USED FOR GLOSSARY:

Burstiner, Irving. **The Small Business Handbook: A Comprehensive Guide to Starting and Running Your Own Business.** New York: Prentice Hall Press, 1989.

Cohen, William A. **The Entrepreneur and Small Business Problem Solver: An Encyclopedia Reference and Guide.** New York: Wiley, 1983.

Davidson, Jeffrey P. **The Marketing Source Book for Small Business.** New York: Wiley, 1989.

Fallek, Max. **How to Set Up Your Own Small Business.** Minneapolis, MN: American Institute of Small Business, 1989.

Friedman, Jack P. **Dictionary of Business Terms.** New York: Barron's, 1987.

Hodgetts, Richard M. & Keel, Pamela. **Topics in Small Business Management.** 2 volumes. 2d ed. Dubuque, IA: Kendall/Hunt Publishing Co., 1982.

The 1991 Business One Irwin Business and Investment Almanac. Homewood, IL: Business One Irwin, 1991.

Munn, Glenn G. **Encyclopedia of Banking and Finance**. 8th ed. Boston: Bankers Publishing Co., 1983.

Oran, Daniel. **The MBA's Dictionary**. Reston, VA: Reston Publishing Co., 1983.

Pratt's Guide to Venture Capital Sources, 1991 Edition. Needham, MA: Venture Economics, Inc., 1991.

Rice, Michael D. **Prentice-Hall Dictionary of Business, Finance, and Law**. Englewood Cliffs, NJ: Prentice-Hall, Inc., 1983.

Rosenberg, Jerry M. **Dictionary of Banking and Financial Services**. New York: Wiley, 1985.

Silvester, James L. **How to Start, Finance, and Operate Your Own Business**. Secaucus, NJ: L. Stuart, 1988.

Terry, John V. **Dictionary for Business and Finance**. Fayetteville, AR: University of Arkansas Press, 1989.

U.S. Small Business Administration. **Small Business Answer Desk Directory**. Washington, DC: Government Printing Office, 1985. SuDoc No. SBA 1.2:An 8.

U.S. Small Business Administration. **The State of Small Business: A report of the President transmitted to the Congress**. Washington, DC: Government Printing Office, 1987 ed. and 1988 ed. SuDoc No. SBA 1.1/2:987 and SBA 1.1/2:988.

A PRACTICAL GUIDE

TO DEVELOPING

THE BUSINESS PLAN

USING THE AVAILABLE RESOURCES OF

THE LOCAL LIBRARY

Patricia A. Peacock, Ed.D.
Regional Small Business Development Center
Rutgers University, Camden, New Jersey
July 1, 1991

Developing the Business Plan

TABLE OF CONTENTS

A BUSINESS PLAN

FOR

YOUR COMPANY NAME

YOUR COMPANY ADDRESS

ANYWHERE, NEW JERSEY 08000

YOUR COMPANY PHONE NUMBER

MONTH, YEAR

This business plan has been prepared by (your name and/or names of all principals here), (your title and/or other principal(s) here). This information and/or data has been compiled by (name(s) of principal(s) involved in this complication here) from documentation made available from (identify source), published in (month, year).

Guidelines:

As the best reference source for the budding entrepreneur, help this author to keep in mind the following hints while compiling the business plan.

1. No two business plans are exactly alike. Do not expect to copy a textbook model and have it suffice. It probably will need to be tailored to meet your specific need.

2. Keep in mind the reader of the finished plan. If this document is to be reviewed by a loan committee, take the time necessary to compile relevant data. It is helpful to have met with the reader, prior to writing the finished plan. Ask the important questions, for example, what is your lending policy? Must this plan reflect a capital infusion on the part of the owner/author? If "yes", how much? What are the terms of a loan? And conditions?

3. Avoid technical jargon. It may make the plan difficult to read and comprehend, and as a result you may lose your reader's interest.

4. Do not make reference to any unnamed people.

5. Be realistic! Most new ventures do not break even in the first year.

6. As the entrepreneur takes notes or makes photocopies of census data or industry trends, remind them to note the publication, date and page.

Note: A business plan may be fashioned to contain all or parts of the following generally accepted elements. Understanding the end goal, entrepreneur's can begin to college the information necessary to address the pertinent topics. (This is very much like seeing the picture on the box of puzzle pieces. While it may take time completing the activity, you at least have an idea of the finished product.) The finished product is 40-50 pages, and includes references and documentation where appropriate.

The Table of Contents Page

Statement of Purpose
The Executive Summary
Table of Contents
The Business

    A.   Description of the Business
    B.   The Product and/or Service
    C.   The Market & Marketing Strategy
    D.   Pricing Policy
    E.   Competition
    F.   Location of the Business
    G.   Management
    H.   Personnel
    I.   Application of Expected Effect of Loan/Investment
    J.   Summary

The Strategic Plan

    A.   Objectives (including Timelines & Budgets)
    B.   Opportunities
    C.   Threats

Financial Data

    A.   Sources & Application of Funding
    B.   Capital Equipment List
    C.   Balance Sheet
    E.   Pro-Forma Income Projections
            Year One (Monthly)
            Year Two (Quarterly)
            Year Three (Quarterly)
            Notes of Explanation (as required)
    F.   Pro-Forma Cash Flow Projections
            Year One (Monthly)
            Year Two (Quarterly)
            Year Three (Quarterly)
            Notes of Explanation (as required)

Supporting Documents

    A.   Personal Resume
    B.   Personal Financial History (3 years of history)
    C.   Job Descriptions
    D.   Company Financial History (if available)
    E.   Credit Report(s) (if available)
    F.   Letters of Reference
    G.   Letters of Intent
    H.   Copies of Lease(s), Contract(s), legal document(s)

Statement of Purpose

Guideline: This is a brief, one paragraph that explains to the reader exactly what this plan has been prepared to do.

The Author Must Explain:

1.   The primary purpose of this plan.
    a. Operational Guide (for internal use)
    b. Financial Proposal (for external interest).

For an Operational Guide:

The Author Must Discuss:

2.   The business structure (sole proprietor, partnership, corporation, or Subchapter S.)
3.   Name the principals.
4.   Briefly explain the product or service.

For a Financial Proposal (include in addition):

5.   Who is asking for the money.
6.   How much is being requested.
7.   What is the money to be used for.
8.   How will the cash infusion help the business.
9.   How will the funds be repaid, and at what rate.
10.   Why the loan or investment makes sense.

Description of the Business

Guideline: The reader will be looking for inconsistencies. Suggest to the entrepreneur that the information presented in this section be consistent with other printed material (Eg: brochures, pamphlets, etc.) from the company. It is a good idea to have gathered sufficient industry data, particularly on market share, before writing this section. Examples: **Small Business: An Information Sourcebook; Small Business Start-Up Index: A Guide to Practical Information Related to Starting a Small Business.**

The Author Must Explain:
1. What is (or will be) this business.
2. What market (the customer base) will be served. How large is this market? (How many customers?) What percentage of the market share will this business capture?
3. Can this venture serve this market better than the existing competition? How?
4. Why has the entrepreneur selected the specific location?
5. What management and other personnel are required and available for the venture?
6. Why will the investment (your money or another's) make this venture profitable?

The Author Must Discuss:

1. The type of business, for example: manufacturing, service, wholesale, import/export, or other.
2. The nature of the product(s) or service(s).
3. The status of the venture: start-up, expansion of a going concern, a take-over.
4. Legal structure: sole proprietor, partnership, corporation.
5. The customers or proposed customers.
6. Why this venture will be profitable.
7. The days and hours of operation (and the date of opening for a new business). If seasonal, be sure to clarify, here.
8. Future expectations, if any.

For a Take Over:

9. When and by whom was the business founded?
10. Why is the owner selling it?
11. What factor(s) determined the purchase price?
12. What is the trend of sales?

Product and/or Service

Guideline: Often the new entrepreneur is in search of a better mousetrap. Thorough research, including the profiles of the industry leaders can be very useful.

The Author Must Discuss:

1. In detail, the product or service that will be sold.

2. If possible, photographs of the product (often available from the distributors or suppliers); the warranties, guarantees, etc., if applicable.

3. If there will be more than one product/service, explain which will generate the greatest income (for example 80% of the revenue). Will one or more items/lines carry others?

4. In detail explain the advantages or benefits that the product/service can provide that are superior or more timely.

The Market

Guideline: The market is defined as the individual or cross section of the population that not only wants the product or service, but can afford to purchase it. Therefore, in general terms, the author must develop a profile of the typical customer. Suggest that the author learn as much as possible about their intended consumer. For example, if they know the publications that are read, recommend that data is sought from their respective marketing staff. Other recommendations - **The Marketing Sourcebook for Small Business** or **Great Ad! Low-Cost Do-It-Yourself Advertising for Your Small Business**.

The Author Must Discuss (in general terms):

1. The apparent total universe (preferably from the experts).
2. A profile of the industry in terms of growth or decline, and at what rate.
3. The projected universe of this venture in relationship to the marketplace.

In addition, the Author Should Define:

4. The customer who makes up this market. Offer as detailed a profile as possible, including, but not limited to: age, gender, profession, income, or any other characteristics that will identify the targeted market segment.
5. The present size of the market (Census data can be very helpful here.)
6. The percent of the market projected for the new venture. (Again, the industry experts may offer a great deal of information.)
7. The market's growth potential.
8. The venture's expected share or loss as the market increases or decreases.

Within every "market" or segment, a specific Marketing Strategy may be required.

The Author Must Discuss:

1. How the product/service will be sold.
2. How the market will come to know the product/service.
3. How product/service loyalty will be developed and maintained.
4. How the venture can satisfy the market.
5. How the owner can expand the market.
6. The advertising and/or public relations tools that will be used, and past history on their success.
7. Specific marketing goals and strategy to be followed.

Pricing

Guideline: Suggest to the entrepreneur that whenever possible, they discuss with the supplier/distributor the recommended retail price, and the range of pricing within the industry. If the new business is a retail establishment, encourage the new owner to do some comparative shopping of their own.

Most importantly, remind the entrepreneur that their integrity is very important. Under no circumstance should they mislead another owner in an effort to secure information.

The Author Must Explain:

1. What formula will be used to price the product or service that includes a fair profit, but at the same time is competitive.?

2. Why will someone pay this price?

3. Is the price competitive?

4. If the price is higher, what special advantages are offered/provided to the customer?

5. Are trade credit terms available? If "yes" under what conditions? What percentage of income may be labeled as bad debt? What information/guidance can the industry provide?

Competition

Guideline: Often the novice entrepreneur truly believes that having built the better mousetrap, they have no competition. Unfortunately, today's consumer is better informed and as a rule, very price conscious. Suggest that information may be gleaned from vendors, employees, or former customers.

The author/new owner must take care in correctly identifying their true competition. Helpful clues include similarity of product line; credentials and/or scope of service.

The Author Must Discuss:

1. The five nearest key competitors. Each is to be listed by name and geographical proximity. Several sentences should be offered to detail the similarity of their market niche.

2. Will the competitive operation be better? If not, why not?

3. What does the competition do or provide that is similar or dissimilar to the author's venture.

4. How is business for the competition? Increasing? Steady? Decreasing?

5. What has the author learned from observing the competition at their location? What insight or guidance, if any, has the competition offered? In the event very little is known about the competition, it is wise to discuss that as well.

6. If the competition is weak, how will this new business fill the "need" created by their weakness?

Location of the Business

Guideline: The State Department of Transportation is a wonderful resource when it comes to information on traffic patterns or count. The information is available at no charge.

The Author Must Discuss:

1. The business address, and the rationale for the decision.

2. The type of zoning use for the address and it's advantage for the business.

3. The physical features of the office/building.

4. The details of the lease or mortgage. The terms of the agreement.

5. Detail any needed renovations, and include written quotations from more than one contractor for the work.

6. Will special licenses or permits be required? Is the neighborhood (location) stable, changing, improving, deteriorating?

7. Have any other sites/locations been considered? If not, why not? Why is this site the most desirable site for the business?

8. Describe the other businesses (if any) in the area?

9. Is this building tailored to your specific needs? Why?

10. Provide a diagram of the building layout. If the layout and traffic pattern will not be similar to others in the industry, explain the advantage or disadvantage.

11. Is parking available? and convenient? What is the traffic pattern? Is it on the "coming home" side of the traffic flow?

12. Can the building be properly secured?

13. How will the location affect operating costs?

14. If the business is homebased, what steps have been taken to ensure privacy and security?

Management

Guidelines: It is a wise idea to recommend that some research be conducted to identify the typical management style of similar going concerns.

The Author Must Discuss:

1. The legal structure intended for the operation, and why. Is it preferred? The only structure that would qualify for insurance?
2. Personal History of each principal:
    a. The business background of each.
    b. Any management experience.
    c. Level of education (formal and informal) and any impact on management ability.
    d. Personal data of each principal, including age, special abilities, interests, reasons for going into business.
    e. Physical stamina and/or limitations that are best suited to the leadership of the venture.
    f. The rationale for success.
    g. A personal financial statement for each principal if the plan is to be used as a financial proposal.
3. Related Work Experience
    a. Explain the specific, hands-on operational experience of each principal for this type of business.
    b. Explain the specific managerial experience of each principal for this type of business.
    c. Do any principals have managerial experience acquired in non-traditional setting, for example, work for a team, club or church? Explain.
    d. If no principal has hands-on operational and/or managerial experience, are there others who have agreed to assume these responsibilities? Include their resumes as supporting documents.
4. Duties & Responsibilities
    a. Who is to do what? Are job descriptions available? (Provide sample in Supporting Documents.)
    b. What is the organizational structure? Who reports to whom? Provide a chart.
    c. How are decisions made? Does the legal structure support this?
    d. List the major operating duties.
5. Salaries, Wages and Hourly Rates
    a. What will management be paid.
6. Other resources available to the business. Discuss respective role and/or responsibilities. E.g: Banker, Attorney, Accountant, Insurance Agent, Consultant, Focus Group, SCORE or ACE representatives, etc.

Personnel

Guidelines: Suggest to the Author that standard job titles and descriptions be used. The **Dictionary of Occupational Titles** may provide useful.

The Author Must Discuss:

1. The personnel needs at the present time, as well as at key times of growth in the future.

2. The skills/qualifications required of each position. (There must be a job description for each position.)

3. Are employees readily available? Discuss recruitment.

4. Will employees be part or full time?

5. Will compensation be as a salary or hourly rate?

6. Will the company provide fringe benefits? If yes, what and at what cost to the company?

7. Will independent contractors be used? If "yes" what is the procedure to check references? Do they have insurance?

8. Will overtime be necessary? Is it covered in the budget?

9. Will training of staff be required? If yes, at what cost to the business? Can the company use any government sponsored programs to reduce the cost of training?

Note: If this company is to be a solo venture, take the time to convincingly explain the owner's skill and talent. Also detail a Plan B, in the event the owner is taken ill, or the demand exceeds capacity for output.

Application and Expected Effect of Loan or Investment

Guidelines: This portion of the Narrative is necessary if this plan is being written to meet the requirements of a lending institution or investor. The author must specify the amount of capital they intend to put into the business. Building on this, the specific dollar sought from the investor and the use of these funds is then discussed. Urge the author to study existing companies, together with the industry norms and ratios. It is also recommended that the author begin by meeting with a loan officer of their Bank of Account. The banker will present the bank's policy on lending money, for example, the required equity investment, and can clarify the loan review process, for example, before a committee.

The Author Must Discuss:

1. How the loan or investment will be spent. The information must be specific, for example: to purchase equipment, to purchase a building; inventory; working capital, etc.
2. A detailed list of items, including specific model name, number, etc. should be provided.
3. Supplier warranties, etc. should be available.
4. The terms of every purchase, including price, deposit, sales tax, installation charge, and/or freight fees must be detailed.
5. How the loan or investment will make the business more profitable.
6. In the event the loan is denied, will the business be operational? What changes if any, must be made? In short, what is the Plan B?

Executive Summary

Guidelines: Often the Executive Summary and the Financials are the only portions of a business plan that are reviewed by members of a loan committee. Therefore, it is important that this summary be specific and to the point.

Description of the Business

1. Business form: proprietorship, partnership or corporation.
2. Type of business: product or service.
3. A definition/description of product or service.
4. Is this a new business? take-over? expansion?
5. When will this business be profitable?
6. When will the business open?
7. Is the business seasonal?
8. What has management learned about this kind of business from outside resources (eg: trade suppliers, banks, trade associations, RMA, D&B, etc.)?

The Market

9. Who exactly is the market (customer base)?
10. How will this venture satisfy the market's "wants"?
11. How will this venture attract and hold their market share?
12. How will the company price its product?

Competition

13. Who are the nearest competitors?
14. How is their business?
15. What has been learned from observing their operation?
16. What strategy will be used to monitor the competition?

Location of the Business

17. What are the location needs for the venture?
18. What kind of building?
19. Is the intended location desirable? Is the building adequate?
20. How will the venture monitor changing demographics?

Management

21. How does the owner's background/business experience help in the establishment of this venture? What are any apparent weaknesses? How will they be compensated?
22. Who are the members of the management team? Why?
23. What are the duties and responsibilities of each member of the management team?
24. Are duties and responsibilities in writing?
25. What additional resources are available to help this venture be successful?

Personnel

26. What are the personnel needs at the time of start-up?
27. What will the needs be in one, two, three years?
28. Are the anticipated wages, salary, fringe benefits, overtime, taxes, etc. available? Competitive?
29. What plans have been made for training? Re-training?

Loan or Investment

30. How will the loan/investment make this business profitable?
31. Is the decision to purchase or to lease - building, equipment, inventory, supplies, etc.
32. Does the venture require this new money to succeed? What factors support the decision to borrow?
33. How is this loan/investment to be applied?

In General

34. How will the owner know when this business is successful? What are the specific benchmarks?
35. Why will this business be a success?

Note: It is important that the author of this plan read, and reread the plan, as though he or she was the investor. Ask yourself these questions. Am I feeling comfortable with the projections? Is the information clearly presented? Does documentation exist beyond the personal belief of the writer? What other information might help explain and/or clarify these objectives?

Strategic Plan

Guideline: There is an old proverb that suggests that unless you know where you are going, you will not know when you have arrived. And while this business plan outlines the broad details of the venture, often, and without warning, a single occurrence can make the difference between success and failure. The "strategic plan" is a short-term (twelve month) set of objectives, as detailed as necessary, to ensure the careful implementation of the business plan.

Objectives

1. List six (or fewer) objectives for the initial twelve month start-up period of this venture. Be as specific as possible.

2. Identify the specific **benchmark** (tangible proof) that will confirm the achievement of each objective.

3. If achievement of the objective will require additional dollars, present a **budget.**

4. Provide a **timetable**. (The use of PERT or Gantt charts or other popular business models is recommended.)

Opportunities: Using specifics explain

1. How the use of this "strategic plan" might profit growth.

2. What are the probable reactions to "opportunity" by our:
    a. Customers
    b. Suppliers
    c. Vendors
    d. Competition

Threats: Using specific examples, explain

1. How events (local, regional, national, interaction) might threaten the profitability of this business. What tools can be used to "forecast" these changes?

2. What are the probable reactions to "threats" by:
    a. Customers
    b. Suppliers
    c. Vendors
    d. Competition

Financial Data

Sources and Applications of Funding

Sources:

Bank Loans:

    1. Mortgage Loan $_____

    2. Term Loan $_____

    3. Reserved Loan $_____

    4. Personal Equity Investment $_____

    5. Outside Equity Investment $_____

    6. Other: _____ $_____

    Total: $_____

Applications:

    1. Purchase Building $_____

    2. Purchase Equipment $_____

    3. Renovations $_____

    4. Inventory $_____

    5. Working Capital $_____

    6. Reserve for Contingencies $_____

    7. Other: _____ $_____

    Total $_____

Capital Equipment List

Major Equipment & Accessories	Model	Cost/List Price
_____	_____	$_____
_____	_____	$_____
_____	_____	$_____
_____	_____	$_____
_____	_____	$_____
	Total:	$_____

Minor Equipment

_____	_____	$_____
_____	_____	$_____
_____	_____	$_____
_____	_____	$_____
	Total:	$_____

Other Equipment

_____	_____	$_____
_____	_____	$_____
_____	_____	$_____
_____	_____	$_____
	Total:	$_____

Historical Records (Required if capital is to support purchase or expansion of an existing business.)

_____	_____	$_____
_____	_____	$_____
_____	_____	$_____
_____	_____	$_____
	Total:	$_____

Balance Sheet

Assets

Current Assets
    Cash $_____
    Accounts Receivable $_____
    Merchandise Inventory $_____
    Supplies $_____
    Prepaid Expenses $_____
Total Current Assets $_____

Fixed Assets
    Fixtures $_____
    Vehicles Receivable $_____
    Equipment $_____
    Leasehold Improvements $_____
    Building $_____
    Land $_____
Total Fixed Assets $_____
Total Assets $_____

Liabilities & Net Worth

Current Liabilities
    Accounts Payable $_____
    Other $_____
Total Current Liabilities $_____

Long Term Liabilities
    Notes Payable $_____
    Bank Loan Payable $_____
    Other Loans Payable $_____
Total Long Term Liabilities $_____

Net Worth:
    Owner Equity $_____

Total Liabilities & Net Worth $_____

Pro-Forma Income Statements
Three Year Summary

	Year I 19____	Year II 19____	Year III 19____
Sales	_____	_____	_____
Less: Cost of Goods Sold	_____	_____	_____
Gross Profit	_____	_____	_____
Operating Expenses:			
Salaries, Wages	_____	_____	_____
Commissions	_____	_____	_____
Payroll Taxes	_____	_____	_____
Advertising & Promotion	_____	_____	_____
Car & Delivery	_____	_____	_____
Gen. Office Administration	_____	_____	_____
Legal & Accounting	_____	_____	_____
Operating Supplies	_____	_____	_____
Bad Debts	_____	_____	_____
Rent	_____	_____	_____
Repairs & Maintenance	_____	_____	_____
Utilities	_____	_____	_____
Insurance	_____	_____	_____
Depreciation	_____	_____	_____
Interest	_____	_____	_____
Miscellaneous	_____	_____	_____
Total Operating Expenses	_____	_____	_____
Profit (Loss) Pre-Tax	_____	_____	_____
Taxes	_____	_____	_____
Net Profit (Loss)	_____	_____	_____

Pro-Forma Cash Flow Projection
Three Year Summary

	Year I 19____	Year II 19____	Year III 19____
Cash Receipts:			
Sales (cash)			
Retail	_____	_____	_____
Wholesale	_____	_____	_____
Accts Receivable	_____	_____	_____
OTHER CASH RECEIPTS	_____	_____	_____
Total Cash Receipts	_____	_____	_____
Cash Disbursements:			
Inventories	_____	_____	_____
Salaries, Wages	_____	_____	_____
Commissions	_____	_____	_____
Outside Labor	_____	_____	_____
Payroll Taxes	_____	_____	_____
Advertising & Promotion	_____	_____	_____
Car & Delivery	_____	_____	_____
Gen. Office Administration	_____	_____	_____
Legal & Accounting	_____	_____	_____
Operating Supplies	_____	_____	_____
Bad Debts	_____	_____	_____
Rent	_____	_____	_____
Repairs & Maintenance	_____	_____	_____
Utilities	_____	_____	_____
Insurance	_____	_____	_____
Taxes & Licenses	_____	_____	_____
Loan Payment (Principle & Interest)	_____	_____	_____
Miscellaneous	_____	_____	_____
Total Cash Disbursements	_____	_____	_____
Net Cash Flow	_____	_____	_____
Cumulative Cash Flow	_____	_____	_____

Break-Even Analysis

Sales: $_____

Cost of Goods Sold: $_____

Gross Profit: $_____

Fixed Expenses: $_____

Net Profit (Loss): $_____

Step 1: Divide Gross Profit by Sales to show percentage relationship.

$$\frac{\text{GROSS PROFIT}}{\text{SALES}} \quad = \quad \text{GROSS PROFIT AS \% OF SALES}$$

Step 2: Divide Fixed Expenses by Profit as % of Sales expressed
         as a decimal (Gross Profit % - 100).

$$\frac{\text{FIXED EXPENSES}}{\text{GROSS PROFIT}} \quad = \quad \text{BREAK-EVEN}$$

Supporting Documents & Additional Notes

Include:

1. Personal Resume of all principals.

2. Job descriptions (current & proposed).

3. Personal Financial Statements (last three (3) years of 1040's).

4. Credit Report(s) (if available).

5. Letters of Reference.

6. Letters of Intent (from prospective clients).

7. Copy of Lease(s) and/or Buy/Sell agreement(s).

8. Copy of any other Agreement(s).

9. Copy of Contract(s).

10. Copy of Proposal(s) (if used as binder for service).

11. Quotation(s) and/or Estimate(s).

12. Any other legal documents relevant to business.

13. Census/Demographic Data.

14. Industry Norms and/or Ratios from noted sources (I.e.: RMA; D&B; Troy's **Almanac**, etc.).

SMALL BUSINESS SOURCES

An annotated bibliography of books, articles,
bibliographies and other materials available as of July 1, 1991 on
starting, financing and operating small businesses

Peter McKay, William Kinyon and Joanne Kosanke

GENERAL

The Business of Business: How 100 Businesses Really Work, by David Horowitz and Dana Shelling. Harper & Row, 1989. 450p. $22.50.
> Brief, entertaining descriptions of the nature of car dealers, travel agencies, supermarkets, hardware stores, florists, video stores, shopping malls, law firms and many more. Topics covered include how many businesses there are in each industry, industry earnings, start-up costs, special problems in each business, number of employees, wages and more.

Business Strategies, by Sidney Kess and Bertil Westin. 4 vols. Looseleaf. Chicago: Commerce Clearing House, 1984-. $560.00/yr.
> This 4 volume looseleaf reporter offers a comprehensive treatment of tax, law and accounting concerns related to business planning. Topical areas covered are: Business Tax Planning, Starting or Expanding a Business, Plant and Equipment, Basic Business Operations, Human Resources, Finances, Intellectual Property, Taking Money Out of the Business, Shareholders Rights and Relations, Accounting, Trade Regulation, Partnerships, Risk Management, Insolvent or Failing Business, Sale-Continuance-Reorganization. Selected articles on business topics are reprinted in volume 3. Monthly updates include "Business Strategies Bulletin" and "Ideas and Trends." Thoroughly indexed.

The Entrepreneur's and Small Business Problem Solver: An Encyclopedic Reference and Guide, by William A. Cohen. 2nd ed. New York: Wiley, 1990. 565p. $58.50.
> The best single volume on small business. Section I contains chapters on the legal and financial aspects of starting a business. Section II covers marketing. Section III concentrates on particular management problems including recruiting employees, patents, copyrights and trademarks, personnel management, security and using computers. Appendixes provide directory listings for small business contact sources. Cohen is the director of the Small Business Institute at California State University, Los Angeles.

"Finding Information on Small Business," by Marydee Ojala. In "The Dollar $ign," **Database** 12(4): 108-111 August 1989.
> Reviews online search terms, strategies and databases useful in finding

information both about operating small businesses and about small business in general.

How to Run a Small Business, by J.K. Lasser Tax Institute. 6th ed. New York: McGraw-Hill, 1989. 314p. $24.95.
A classic text on managing a small business.

Making Your Small Business a Success, by G. Howard Poteet. Blue Ridge Summit, PA: Liberty Hall Press, 1991. 224p. pbk. $17.95.
A collection of articles written by business experts commissioned by the SBA on management strategies for small business owners.

The Small Business Information Handbook, by Gustav Berle. New York: Wiley, 1990. 256p. $19.95.
A miscellany of terms, facts, concepts, tips, strategies, associations and contacts of interest to small business. Arranged alphabetically. A sampling of entries includes: Advertising Media Selection, Assets, Bank Loans, Cable TV, Coentrepreneurs, FAX, Growth, Incubators, National Retail Hardware Association, Real Estate, Red Tape, Selling a Business, Startup Advice, Success, Waste Disposal, Women in Business.

BIBLIOGRAPHIES, INDEXES & SOURCEBOOKS

"Fueling the Entrepreneurial Dream: Small Business Resources," by Mark Leggett and Betty Tomeo. In "The Alert Collector," edited by Tony Stankus. **RQ** 29(3):341-346 Spring 1990.
The article discusses useful core sources of information for the entrepreneur. Leggett and Tomeo are business librarians at the Indianapolis-Marion County Public Library.

Planning and Funding for Small Business: A Bibliography. by Dava P. James. Monticello, IL: Vance Bibliographies, 1990. 5p. $3.00.
A selection of citations to articles in business magazines appearing between 1985 and 1989 on financing and managing small businesses.

Small Business: An Information Sourcebook, by Cynthia C. Ryans. (Oryx Sourcebook Series in Business and Management) Phoenix: Oryx Press, 1987. 286p. $45.00.

> Annotated entries provide information on numerous sources covering all aspects of starting and operating a small business. A "Core Library Collection" is included. Appendixes include a directory of publishers, a list of SBA programs and field offices. Ryans edits the "Resources" column in the **Journal of Small Business Management.**

"Small Business Matters." Library Journal 115(5): 48-49 March 15, 1990. By Lisa Woznicki, Joyce Bernstein and Kathleen S. Reif.

> An annotated bibliography of 35 titles that are frequently used by Baltimore County librarians in their small business information centers.

Small Business Sourcebook, edited by Carol A. Schwartz. 2 vols. 4th ed. Detroit, MI: Gale Research, 1990. 2000p. $199.00.

> "An annotated guide to live and print sources of information and assistance for 194 specific small businesses, with a detailed listing of similar sources for the small business community in small businesses, with a detailed listing of similar sources for the small business community in general." This sourcebook makes everyone's list of core resources. Thoroughly indexed.

Small Business Start-Up Index: A Guide to Practical Information Related to Starting a Small Business, edited by Michael Madden. Detroit, Mich.: Gale Research, 1990- (three times a year). $125.00/yr.

> An index to sources of information for starting hundreds of small businesses. It covers several hundred periodicals as well as books, book chapters, audio-visual materials and pamphlets. A "Sources Used" section provides complete ordering information.

"Sources of Information About Small Business." Journal of Accountancy 165(6): 144+ June 1988. Compiled by Karen Hegge Neloms.

> Over one hundred entries list sources of business information on topics including accounting, auditing and taxation, management, marketing and advertising, business planning and start-up, buying and selling a business, selecting computers for small businesses, general information sources and journals. Neloms is director of the AICPA's library services division.

BUSINESS PLANS

The Ernst & Young Business Plan Guide, by E.S. Siegel, L.A. Schultz, B.R. Ford and D.C. Carney. New York: Wiley, 1990. 336p. $29.95.

> Elucidates the researching, writing and presentation of a business plan. Discusses how to tailor the business plan for the intended reviewer. Contains a detailed sample plan.

How to Prepare and Present a Business Plan, by Joseph R. Mancuso. Englewood, NJ: Prentice-Hall, 1990. pbk. $14.95.

> The business plan is vital to raising money for a growing company. Most business plans are written by entrepreneurs seeking venture capital. It forces the business person to be objective, critical, and unemotional about the business. Once finished, it also aids in managing the business and in accomplishing one's objectives. Mancuso maintains that the greatest value of the plan is to the entrepreneur who prepares it.

How to Write Your Own Business Plan Project Kit, by Max Fallek. Minneapolis, MN: American Institute of Small Business, 1989. 3v. 187p. $85.00.

> The kit is made up of three components. The first section explains why a business plan is important and provides step-by-step instructions for preparing a plan. The second section provides a business start-up example. The third section provides the complete text of a plan based on the example.

FINANCIAL RATIOS

Almanac of Business and Industrial Financial Ratios, edited by Leo Troy. Englewood Cliffs, NJ: Prentice-Hall. Annual. $49.95.

> Provides financial and operating ratios for more than 150 lines of business including banks and other financial institutions. Statistics are based on IRS tax returns.

Financial Studies of the Small Business. Winter Haven, FL: Financial Research Associates. Annual.

> Financial and operating rations are provided for over 50 lines of small capitalization businesses (under $1,000,000).

Industry Norms and Key Business Ratios. Dun & Bradstreet Credit Services. New York. Annual. $267.50.

> Provides financial ratios for more than 800 lines of business arranged by Standard Industrial Classification Code.

RMA Annual Statement Studies. Philadelphia, PA: Robert Morris Associates. Annual. $95.00.

> This is an annual series of ratios for industries in selected Standard Industrial Classification 4-digit categories. The introduction provides good definitions of the significant ratios. There is a subject index and a sources bibliography. Starting with 1990 data is provided by sales volume as well as asset size.

FINANCE

The Arthur Young Guide to Raising Venture Capital, by G. Steven Burrill and Craig T. Norback. Blue Ridge Summit, PA: Liberty House, 1988. 252 p. $24.95.
> Presents an overview of venture capital financing, where to find venture capital, how to prepare a business plan, meeting with venture capitalists and how to negotiate a deal. An appendix lists and discusses alternatives to venture capital. A directory of venture capital firms in the U.S. and Canada is included.

Buying In: A Complete Guide to Acquiring a Business or Professional Practice, by Lawrence W. Tuller. Blue Ridge Summit, PA: Liberty Hall Press, 1990. 310p. $24.95.
> Examines in detail how to purchase an existing business. Includes an assessment of the decision to purchase rather than start-up a business, how to negotiate and finance the purchase, and what to do after the acquisition.

Credit Considerations: Financial and Credit Characteristics of Selected Industries. Philadelphia, PA: Robert Morris Associates, 1986. $80.00.
> Written from the lender's point of view, 50 articles provide an overview of 44 industries. The major industry groups covered are: Agricultural Credits, Manufacturers, Real Estate/Contractors, Retailers, Wholesalers, Service Companies and other Industries. "Each article includes a description of the industry; financial information; an analysis of potential credit risks; typical financing, loan structure, and repayment; and collateral unique to a particular type of business." Also available are: **Credit Considerations Supplement** ($23.00) and **Credit Considerations Volume II** ($110.00) which covers an additional 37 industries.

The Ernst & Young Guide to Raising Capital, by D.R. Garner. New York: Wiley, 1990. 336p. $29.95.
> Explains a variety of financing methods: venture capital, leasing, franchising, government loans, management buyouts, going public, employee stock ownership plans, and financing options for troubled companies.

Get That Business Loan: Convince Your Banker to Say Yes, by Harley A. Rennhoff. Gretna, LA.: Pelican, 1987. 163p. pbk. $12.95.
> Rennhoff writes from the viewpoint of a banker and loan officer in hopes of easing the path of the would-be borrower. He gives two basic rules: 1) Do your homework and be prepared, and 2) Don't be intimidated by your banker. Included are several case studies.

Guerrilla Financing: Alternative Techniques to Finance Any Small Business, by Bruce Blechman and J. Conrad Levinson. Boston: Houghton Mifflin, 1991. 343p. $19.95.
> Explores unconventional methods of financing a small business.

Hands-On Financial Controls for Your Small Business, by Cecil J. Bond. Blue-Ridge Summit, PA: Liberty Hall Press, 1991. 224p. $27.95.

Offers detailed treatment of financial management for the small business including bank financing, budgeting, controlling employee costs, purchasing, scheduling, setting prices, sales management, managing accounts receivable and controlling maintenance costs.

How to Get a Business Loan (Without Signing Your Life Away), by Joseph R. Mancuso. New York: Prentice-hall, 1990. 270p. pbk. $12.95.

A complete guide to obtaining a loan, written in the matchless Mancuso style.

How to Start, Finance and Manage Your Own Small Business, by Joseph R. Mancuso. Englewood Cliffs, NJ: Prentice-Hall, 1990. pbk. $16.95.

A primer on establishing, funding and running a business enterprise.

Lending to Different Industries, Volume 1, Second Edition. Robert Morris Associates, 1990-. $70.00.

Contains articles (many updated) that first appeared in the **Journal of Commercial Bank Lending** that analyze lending considerations for restaurants, radio stations, professional athletes, automobile dealerships, the fast food industry, the hotel industry and many more. Also available: **Lending to Different Industries**, Volume 2, Second Edition ($70.00).

Pratt's Guide to Venture Capital Sources, by Venture Economics Staff. Phoenix, AZ: Oryx Press, 1990. 750p. $125.00. Annual.

The first section features articles on the venture investment process. The heart of this book is a listing of over 800 venture capital companies in the U.S. and Canada. Arranged by state and province, each entry gives name, address, telephone number, management, contact person, type of firm, affiliation, project preferences, minimum investment, geographical preference, industry preference. There is an industry preference index.

Raising Money: Venture Funding & How to Get It, by Ronald E. Merrill and Gaylord E. Nichols. New York: American Management Association, 1990. 283p. $24.95.

A guide to raising money in the venture capital market. Covers gathering marketing information, preparing the business plan and executive summary, financing options, the financing process, making a presentation and negotiating the deal.

Raising Start-Up Capital for Your Company, by Gustav Berle. New York: Wiley, 1990. 244p. $49.95.

Covers private sources of financing, government-assisted financing and miscellaneous other topics pertinent to financing a small business.

SBA Loans: A Step-by-Step Guide, by Patrick D. O'Hara. New York: Wiley, 1989. 230p. $39.95.
> Explains the two basic loans (Guaranty and Direct) provided by the Small Business Administration and details each step of the application and review process. Appendixes include a sample business plan with financial projections and addresses of SBA field offices. The focus is on California.

The Small Business Financial Planner, by Gregory R. Glau, New York: Wiley, 1989. 210p. $29.95.
> Covers financial management of small businesses, including measures of profitability, liquidity, cash flow analysis, business ratios, cost accounting, leverage, inventory and accounts receivable management, break-even analysis and budgeting. Includes a glossary and a bibliography of magazine articles and books.

Start-Up Money: Raise What You Need for Your Small Business, by Jennifer Lindsey. New York: Wiley, 1989. 247p. $39.95.
> Provides information on determining how much capital to raise, preparing the financial package, investigating primary and secondary sources of capital as well as self-financing/blind pools, balancing debt and equity. Treatment focuses on raising $100,000 or less. Appendixes.

IMPORT/EXPORT

A Basic Guide to Exporting. U.S. Department of Commerce, International Trade Administration, 1986.
> This introduction to exporting reviews what decisions must be made, what information is needed to make them and where to get the necessary information.

Building an Import/Export Business, Revised and Expanded, by K.D. Weiss. New York: Wiley, 1991. 288p. $29.95.
> Analyzes import/export opportunities, explains how to conduct international transactions, discusses setting up the business, choosing suppliers, targeting markets and writing a business plan. Includes an evaluation of trading opportunities with the European Economic Community and Eastern Europe.

The Export Trading Company Guidebook, Revised Edition. U.S. Department of Commerce. International Trade Administration, 1987.
> Provides information on the workings and advantages of establishing or using an export trading company.

Exporter's Guide to Federal Resources for Small Business, Revised Edition. Interagency Task Force on Trade, 1988.
> Descriptions of the major federal programs designed to assist small business owners to export. Identifies those agencies able to provide technical assistance.

Import/Export: A Guide for Growth, Profits and Market Share, by Howard R. Goldsmith. Prentice-Hall, 1989. $21.95.
> This is a practical guide to the import/export business for small and medium-sized companies.

Profitable Exporting: A Complete Guide to Marketing Your Products Abroad, by John S. Gordon and J.R. Arnold. Wiley, 1988. $45.00.
> This book guides the business person through the exporting process. The authors believe that companies with limited resources can succeed in export.

The World Is Your Market: An Export Guide for Small Business, edited by William A. Delphos. Washington, D.C.: Braddock Communications, 1990.
> Deals with the basics - finding customers, export financing, getting the product to market, and federal, state and private sector organizations offering export assistance.

MARKETING & ADVERTISING

Advertising and Public Relations for a Small Business. Fifth edition. D. Bellavance Agency, 323 Beacon St., Boston, MA 02116 (617-262-0411). February 1991. 100p. $16.95.
> A handbook explaining how to plan a promotional campaign, including selection of media, purchasing advertising space and getting publicity.

"Did You See My Ad?": When, Why, and How to Advertise the Small Business, by Larry Semon. Andover, MA: Brick House Publishing Co., 1988. 128p. pbk. $12.95.
> A guide to advertising in any medium. Newspapers, television, radio, direct mail, yellow pages, and other forms of advertising are discussed, with emphasis on what the small business should and should not do in each medium.

Guerrilla Marketing Attack: New Strategies, Tactics, and Weapons for Winning Big Profits for Your Small Business, by Jay Conrad Levinson. Boston: Houghton Mifflin, 1989. 224p. $17.95.
> A discussion of the strategies and tactics of marketing a business. Directed at laymen who have little knowledge or experience in marketing, this source covers such topics as marketing "weapons," marketing tactics to consider, effective media use, and marketing myths. Emphasis is placed on the "real world" of marketing and how the small business owner should react to it.

Great Ad! Low-Cost Do-It-Yourself Advertising For Your Small Business, by Carol Wilkie Wallace. Blue Ridge Summit, PA: Liberty Hall Press, 1990. 340p. $32.95.

> Offers a commonsense approach to advertising for small business based on adopting the customer's point of view. The first section explains how to analyze one's own business, customers, and the competition. The second section details media planning. The third section explores how to develop a professional, consistent advertising campaign. Checklists are included on each topic. Final chapters deal with obtaining publicity and the legal aspects of advertising.

The Marketing Sourcebook for Small Business, by Jeffrey P. Davidson. New York: Wiley, 1989. 325p. $24.95.

> A guide to marketing for the small business. Contains a valuable discussion of the theory and the "why" of the marketing process. Includes names, addresses, and other data about a variety of information sources.

START-UP

The Field Guide to Starting a Business, by Stephen M. Pollan and Mark Lavine. New York, Fireside Book: Simon & Schuster, 1990. 292p. pbk. $9.95.

> Part I covers basic problems and principles every entrepreneur needs to know. Part II builds on the early chapters and deals with specific situations and businesses. A step-by-step guide.

Free Help from Uncle Sam to Start Your Own Business (or expand the one you have), by William M. Alarid and Gustav Berle. Santa Maria, CA: Puma Publishing Col., 1989. Rev. ed. 208p. pbk. $11.95.

> Descriptions of over 100 Government programs which can be of assistance in starting a business. The programs included can provide financial assistance, instructional activities, consulting, or access to or use of facilities and properties. For each program the book lists the federal agency, the agency's objectives, types of assistance, uses and use restrictions, eligibility requirements, and information contacts.

How to Set Up Your Own Small Business, by Max Fallek. Minneapolis, MN: American Institute of Small Business, 1990. 2v. $149.95.

> Fallek covers comprehensively the steps in starting and running a small business based on the results of a business institute study. There are lists of resources for information. Included is an excellent chapter on business plans. Written with the help of real small business owners, this is practical, basic and comprehensible.

Legal Handbook for Small Business, by Marc J. Lane. AMACOM, 1989. Revised edition. 250p. $19.95.

Covers the legal aspects of setting up and operating a small business. Topics include structuring the enterprise, accounting, intellectual property, commercial law, credit, dealing with professional accountants, lawyers and bankers, insurance, taxes, liability issues, and going public.

The McGraw-Hill Guide to Starting Your Own Business: A Step-by-Step Blueprint for the First-Time Entrepreneur, by Stephen C. Harper. New York: McGraw-Hill, 1990. 203p. $19.95.

Part 1 examines the prerequisites for start-up survival and success. Part 2 discusses preparing the business plan. Part 3 deals with the ABCs of financing and alternatives to starting from scratch.

Planning and Financing the New Venture, by Jeffry A. Timmons. Acton, Mass.: Brick House, 1990. 188p. $24.95.

Focuses on preparing a business plan and obtaining financing to start a new business. This is the third book in a series on entrepreneurship. **The Entrepreneurial Mind** (1989) examines what makes a successful entrepreneur. **New Business Opportunities** (1990) details the process of selecting and evaluating new business ideas.

Small Time Operator: How to Start Your Own Small Business, Keep Your Books, Pay Your Taxes, & Stay Out of Trouble: A Guide and Workbook, by Bernard Kamoroff. Laytonville, CA: Bell Springs Pub., 1990. Revised edition. 192p. pbk. $12.95.

A practical introduction to the major issues involved in starting a business. Written in layman's language, this source gives details on "how-to-do-it" plus examples of actual small businesses and their experiences in starting up.

Starting and Operating a Business in (name of state), by Michael D. Jenkins. Oasis Press, 1989-. (3-ring binder). $29.95.

A self-help guide to financial, legal, and tax considerations involved in starting a business. A separate volume is planned for each state, with help from experts in the respective state. Each edition includes sections applicable to small business in any state, and a section pertaining to the particular state.

Starting and Operating a Home-Based Business, by David R. Eyler. New York: Wiley, 1990. 256p. pbk. $14.95.

Discusses home-based businesses. Chapters cover the advantages and disadvantages of working at home, furnishing a home office, selecting computers and telecommunications equipment, various kinds of businesses, legal, tax and insurance aspects of home businesses. Includes a bibliography.

Starting Up Your Own Business: Expert Advice From the U.S. Small Business Administration, edited by G. Howard Poteet. Blue Ridge Summit, PA: Liberty Hall Press, 1991. 269p. pbk. $19.60.

A compilation of publications from the SBA on starting, financing and managing a small business including preparation of business plans.

Your Home Business Can Make Dollars and Sense, by Jo Frohbieter-Mueller. Radnor, Penn.: Chilton, 1990. 273p. pbk. $16.95.

A primer on starting a home business. Includes information on selecting the right business, a list of home business possibilities, surveying the market, choosing an organizational form, funding, financial management, pricing, advertising, taxes and insurance.

Your Own Shop: How to Open & Operate a Successful Retail Business, by Ruth Jacobson. Blue Ridge Summit, PA: Liberty Hall Press, 1991. 214p. pbk. $12.95.

Covers all facets of choosing, financing, locating and operating a retail store. Jacobson is a former executive director of SCORE (Service Corps of Retired Executives Association).

NON-LIBRARY INFORMATION SOURCES FOR SMALL BUSINESS

Deborah Sommer
Director, The SBDC Connection
University of Georgia
Athens, GA

BUSINESS ASSISTANCE PROGRAMS OR ORGANIZATIONS

FEDERAL AND STATE LEVEL

Small Business Development Centers - Currently over 700 offices nationwide in each state, Puerto Rico, and the Virgin Islands. Services include seminars, learning centers, conferences, and business counseling. Most services are free of charge or available for minimal costs.

Small Business Institutes - Currently over 500 nationwide located at Universities. Offer extensive counseling utilizing students.

SCORE (Service Corps of Retired Executives) - Locally-chartered volunteer organizations which provide problem-solving assistance to small businesses. SCORE matches counseling experience with client needs. To locate a chapter near you, contact the national SCORE association, (202) 653-6279, or your District or Regional SBA Office.

U.S. Small Business Administration - The SBA offers the small business owner a variety of services and programs. It also serves as the advocate for small business within the federal government. Assistance for individuals is best directed to the District or Regional Office in your area (a list of these can be found in the **Small Business Sourcebook** or the **U.S. Government Manual)**. Major divisions of the SBA are:

Business Development

Finance and Investment (Business Loans)

Procurement Assistance

Veterans Affairs Office

Innovation, Research and Technology

Advocacy (Small Business Answer Desk 1-800-827-5722)

Minority Small Business and Capital Ownership

International Trade Assistance

Women's Business Ownership

Many other federal government agencies have an office of small and disadvantaged business. Most state governments also have an agency in place specifically for small business or have an office within their larger commerce or economic development department. See **STATE YELLOW PAGES**.

PRIVATE SECTOR

The Chamber of Commerce of the U.S. has a Small Business Programs Office which acts as a central clearinghouse about small business resources throughout the state and local chambers in the U.S. (202) 659-6000.

The National Federation of Independent Business (NFIB) - the nation's largest organization exclusively representing small and independent businesses. Provides a variety of services from surveys on economic trends to lobbying. Publishes several newsletters and other publications. (202) 554-9000.

National Small Business United - An organization made up of regional small business groups. Offers educational programs, networking, lobbying, and business assistance. Publishes a monthly newsletter. (202) 293-8830.

For other organizations and trade associations for specific types of small businesses or business owners consult the **SMALL BUSINESS SOURCEBOOK** or the **ENCYCLOPEDIA OF ASSOCIATIONS**.

REFERENCE SOURCES FOR IDENTIFYING NON-LIBRARY CONTACTS AND RESOURCES

Census Catalog and Guide. Washington, DC: GPO, annual.

Directories in Print. Detroit, MI: Gale Research, 1991.

Encyclopedia of Associations. Detroit, MI: Gale Research, annual.

Federal Yellow Book and **State Yellow Book.** Washington, DC: Monitor Publishing Co., quarterly.

Government Giveaways for Entrepreneurs. by Matt Lesko. Chevy Chase, MD: Information USA, Inc., 1991.

Inventing and Patenting Sourcebook: How to Sell and Protect Your Ideas. Detroit, MI: Gale Research, 1990.

Lesko's Info-Power Data Updates for Infomaniacs (formerly **The Data Informer**). Chevy Chase, MD: Information USA, Inc., monthly newsletter.

The Small Business Sourcebook. Detroit, MI: Gale Research, 1991.

State Data and Database Finder. Chevy Chase, MD: Information USA, Inc.

U.S. Department of Commerce. Bureau of the Census. "Telephone Contacts List." (301) 763-4100.

U.S. Government Manual. Washington, DC: U.S. Government Printing Office, annual.

MARKETING THE LIBRARY TO SMALL BUSINESS
CONTACT NAMES & ADDRESSES

Nancy Sherwin
Porter Public Library
Westlake, OH

Baltimore County Public Library
320 York Road
Towson, MD 21204-5179
(301) 887-6100
Contact: Kathleen S. Reif
Coordinator, Marketing & Programming

Cleveland Hts.-University Hts. Public Library
Contact: Nancy H. Sherwin
Public Services Librarian
Porter Public Library
27333 Center Ridge Road
Westlake, OH 44145

Cleveland Public Library
325 Superior Avenue
Cleveland, OH 44114-1271
(216) 623-2927
Contact: Julius Bremer
Head, Business, Economics & Labor Dept.

Fresno County Free Library
2420 Mariposa Street
Fresno, CA 93721
(209) 488-3191
Contact: Steve Fjeldsted
Business Services Librarian

Indianapolis-Marion County Public Library
40 East St. Clair
Indianapolis, IN 46206-0211
(317) 269-1772
Contact: James R. Cannon
Business, Science & Technology Division

Kansas City, Kansas Public Library
Contact: David Lane
formerly Business Librarian at KCKPL
current address: 4648 Aldrich Ave. S.
Minneapolis, MN 55409
(612) 334-4422

Multnomah County Library
205 N E Russell Street
Portland, OR 97212-3708
(503) 221-7724
Contact: June Mikkelsen
Director of Central Library

Newport Beach Public Library
856 San Clemente Drive
Newport Beach, CA 92660
(714) 644-3188
Contact: Thomas L. Johnson
Assistant City Librarian

Porter Public Library
27333 Center Ridge Road
Westlake, OH 44145
(216) 871-2600
Contact: Nancy H. Sherwin
Public Services Librarian

Prince George's County Memorial Library
6532 Adelphi Road
Hyattsville, MD 20782
(301) 699-3500
Contact: Judith C. Cooper
Development Officer

Toledo-Lucas County Public Library
325 Michigan Street
Toledo, OH 43624
(419) 259-5244
Contact: Galen Avery
Government Procurement Center

Tulsa City-County Library System
400 Civic Center
Tulsa, OK 74103-3822
(918) 596-7977
Contact: Robert W. Sears